D1242819

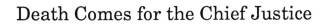

Death Comes for the Chief Justice

John Potts Slough, the obstreperous chief justice of the New Mexico Supreme Court, 1866–1867. *Courtesy of Museum of New Mexico. Neg. no. 50542.*

Death Comes for the Chief Justice

The Slough-Rynerson Quarrel and
Political Violence in New Mexico

Gary L. Roberts

University Press of Colorado

The University Press of Colorado is a cooperative publishing enterprise
supported, in part, by Adams State College, Colorado State University,
Fort Lewis College, Mesa State College, Metropolitan State College, University of Colorado, University of Northern Colorado, University of
Southern Colorado, and Western State College.

The paper used in this publication meets the minimum requirements of
the American National Standard for Information Sciences—Permanence
of Paper for Printed Library Materials.
ANSI Z39.48–1984

Library of Congress Cataloging-in-Publication Data

Roberts, Gary L., 1942–
    Death comes for the chief justice: the Slough-Rynerson
quarrel and political violence in New Mexico / Gary L. Roberts. — 1st ed.
        p.   cm.
    Includes abebliographical references.
    ISBN 0-87081-212-2
    1. Rynerson, William Logan — Trials, litigation, etc.   2.
Trials (Assassination) — New Mexico.   3. Slough, John
Potts, d. 1867 — Assassination.   4. Political crimes and
offenses — New Mexico — History.   5. New Mexico — Politics and givernment — 1848–1950.   I. Title.
KF223.R96R63 1990
306.2'0972 — dc20   90-10967
                                                        CIP

To loving memory of my brother,
Michael Lynn Roberts (1949–1985)

Contents

Preface

The history of New Mexico is a rich tapestry filled with images that elevate the human spirit and testify to the ability of people of different cultures to find understanding among themselves and to build something lasting and good. In the land of *poco tiempo,* Indians, Hispanos, and Anglos together have built a fascinating and vibrant place that beckons to those who seek a haven of spirit and beauty where tradition and progress can coexist, each with mutual respect for the other.

But that intricate weaving of timeless charm was not fashioned in a storybook fantasy of harmony and cooperation. The peculiar convergence of diverse cultures in New Mexico inevitably meant conflict in an environment that for a surprisingly long time gave little real advantage to any of the contending groups. Conflict gave texture and definition to the changing society as men and women of contrasting values sought to find accommodations and to protect divergent lifeways. But conflict also bred pain and bitterness, which ultimately left a blood-red thread of violence in the fabric of New Mexico history that — rightly or wrongly — marked the political order with an unenviable reputation for lawlessness, mayhem, and assassination.

On December 15, 1867, William Logan Rynerson, a member of New Mexico's legislature, shot and mortally wounded John Potts Slough, the chief justice of the territory's Supreme Court. The circumstances of Slough's death were sensational because they involved two public officials. More importantly, Slough's killing also seemed to legitimize assassination as a political tactic: Political murders flourished in New Mexico over the next half-century. This distinctive form of violence set New Mexico apart from other areas of the Southwest (such as Texas, where overall levels of violence were as high or higher than they were in New Mexico) and from the main-stream patterns of American violence.

This book is a detailed reconstruction of the events sur-rounding the death of John Slough. It is both a case study of violence on the American frontier and an effort to understand the peculiar character of political turmoil in New Mexico within the broad context of violence in American history. The portrait of New Mexico violence that emerges from the Slough-Rynerson tragedy deviates in important ways from conventional interpretations that stress the territory's fron-tier environment or its ethnic conflict (both of which occurred elsewhere without a corresponding history of political assas-sination). Rather, the circumstances of the Slough murder suggest a series of generalizations that may well have appli-cations far beyond New Mexico.

First, violence is the product of condition, not of place. Classic interpretations of violence have almost universally attributed the United States's violent strain to the frontier experience, to an unrelieved chain of Indian wars, outlawry, brigandage, and vigilante justice in the conquest of succes-sive "wests." According to this view, the pattern of violence in association with the westward movement and a frontier myth that transformed violence into a necessary and regenerative force ultimately infected the American character so thor-oughly that the strain of violence survived the passing of the frontier into the twentieth century. Other scholars have ar-gued persuasively that violence has been more of an urban problem than a frontier problem, that cities have posed a greater threat to life and limb than has "new country."

In both variations, the emphasis has been upon *where* violence occurred historically. Curiously, this preoccupation with place obscures the more obvious conclusion that violence proceeds from a set of conditions that may exist in any physical environment, including frontier hamlets and big cities. This approach, though no less environmental than the place-based interpretations, transcends place to argue that when violence did occur on the frontier it occurred for essentially *the same reasons* that it occurs elsewhere. If this is true, the task is to determine what conditions encourage violence and then to document the environmental milieux conducive to violence.

Second, violence is most likely to occur when the authority structure (government, social system, or any other formal or informal mechanism of social control) is insufficient, when the authority structure is undermined by inefficiency, corruption, or a lack of public support, or when the authority structure itself feels so threatened that it takes action to defend itself. Internalized norms or a consensus on right and wrong behavior probably sustain order better than other control systems, including government — which is not always effective or efficient as an instrument of social control. In the case of New Mexico, the feeble territorial government was incapable of exerting real authority over the far-flung, multi-ethnic, and isolated settlements; but, equally important, no shared conception of acceptable behavior had emerged. Hence, Indian wars, criminal activity, vigilantism, and local conflicts growing out of disputes over land or ethnic differences were commonplace. The government's failure to respond effectively to the disorder created disillusionment, contempt, and mistrust of the law and its representatives, while differing norms among the groups bred conflict.

Third, violence will be justified when it can be construed to be in the interest of the community, that is, that group to which individuals owe first loyalty. This generalization holds both for groups that perceive themselves to be oppressed by the authority structure and for the authority structure itself when it sees its own interests threatened. Violence is justified on this basis whenever a serious threat to community is perceived, and it rarely matters whether the threat is real or imagined. Again, this condition may exist in any environment, rural or urban, historical or contemporary. New Mexico's fragmented population and multiple interests guaranteed that not everyone saw the interest of the community in the same light. Each group defined "community" in terms of its particular interests and acted upon that definition, not on the basis of some larger, integrated community.

Fourth, assassination is more characteristic of traditional societies in which the political system is experiencing fundamental structural changes at variance with traditional practices than of modern societies with well-developed democratic institutions or of highly coercive societies. New Mexico had a long history of weak government. Government under Spain and Mexico was autocratic but not truly authoritarian. After the territory was acquired by the United States, efforts to implement the new republican order struggled to find acceptance among people who resisted the changes. New Mexico's most violent years paralleled the adaptations of traditional Hispanic cultural norms to a new Anglo-American order. Government that was neither truly coercive nor democratically permissive failed to win the respect of the populace.

Finally, assassination is directly related to systemic frustration reflected in levels of violence, minority discontent, disrespect for the authority structure, and a perception of oppression. Instability was the norm in New Mexico until late in the territorial period. Violence of almost every kind thrived in New Mexico. The Hispanic population maintained traditional ways in defiant evasion of change or chafed under Anglo influences with a bitter knowledge that they had lost the freedom to live as they chose, while Anglos pursued a "root-hog-or-die" philosophy based upon economic gain and political manipulation. The general instability created suspicions that delayed the growth of a strong party system and transformed politics into a game of thrust and parry in which politicians from different factions were not merely opponents but bitter enemies out to destroy each other.

This book is an effort to treat violence in context. The frontier experience, in particular, has created an illusion that American violence was somehow exceptional, somehow excessive in comparison to other nations — when the weight of recent scholarship tends to show that the most unique aspect of American violence has always been its mythology. This mythology has been used variously to defend and to criticize (from both the Left and the Right) American life. It also engendered a "Wild West" mentality that trivialized the study of Western violence and obscured its legitimacy as a field of study. Perhaps most importantly, the frontier myth evolved as the country evolved, giving contemporary validation to the notion of exceptionalism in virtually every period and, in fact, contributing directly to the reality of violence in American life down to the present.

Violence in New Mexico was an outward manifestation of deepseated social, economic, and political tensions, rather than an exercise in *machismo* or an expression of a Wild West syndrome. Real differences lay at the heart of the violence; within the context of the political infighting of the times, violence "made sense" as an instrument in the struggle for power. Within the political order of territorial New Mexico, violence was for a time both rational and functional. However senseless, morally reprehensible, and wrongminded the Slough-Rynerson quarrel appears through the lenses of rational judgment, it was an understandable outcome of basic human drives and emotions in general and of political power struggles in particular. Apparently, violence is a natural part of the political continuum that cannot be dismissed out of hand as aberration. This premise renders violence all the more terrifying — and if it be true, the present generation is not too far removed in time and space to profit from the telling of this particular story of violence, death, and politics.

GARY L. ROBERTS
Tifton, Georgia

Acknowledgements

I met John Slough quite by accident and at the time gave him little thought. He was simply a minor character who I encountered in my quest to understand a more sanguinary example of American violence, the Sand Creek Massacre. I expected to mention him and move on, but even in that story he assumed a larger role than I had imagined. When I left him in the aftermath of Sand Creek, discharged from the army and out of work, I wondered what had happened to him. When I discovered that he had been killed by William Logan Rynerson, a personage I remembered from my interest in yet another violent enterprise — the Lincoln County War — I began a file on the topic and hoped that I would have a chance to someday pursue it.

The chance came in the autumn of 1971 in a coffee shop at Stapleton International Airport in Denver, Colorado. I was returning home from the annual meeting of the Western History Association and fell into conversation with Gustav L. Seligmann, professor of history at the University of North Texas and a diligent student of New Mexico history. Gus was putting together a session on political violence in New Mexico for the next year's meeting at Yale University. He had a distinguished group already collected for the task, but he needed another paper. I told him of my interest in Slough, and the deal was struck.

During the next year, most of the research that undergirds this work was done. A critical break came when the late Clinton P. Anderson, a distinguished United States senator from New Mexico and himself a student of his state's history, allowed me to visit his Washington office and to examine and take notes from Herman H. Heath's letterbook. This inside view of patronage politics in New Mexico proved critical, especially after the Arizona Historical Society provided copies of Jose Francisco Chaves's letters to Heath for the same period. The correspondence of these two prominent actors in New Mexcio's political drama provided crucial insights.

Fortunately, I also fell heir to the generosity of a delightful and meticulous researcher named Jane C. Sanchez. I had read her 1966 article from the *New Mexico Historical Review* on Robert Byington Mitchell's conflict with the New Mexico legislature in 1868, and I wrote her hoping that she might be able to direct me to sources. Instead, she opened her research to me and answered endless questions with grace and patience. She saved me countless hours of research time and guided me patiently through the maze of New Mexico politics until I felt that I could at least identify the issues and players.

By the time the original paper was presented at the Yale Conference of the Western History Association in 1972, Slough's murder had become an intriguing window to the nature of American violence, and insights I gained there I used later in several essays and in my dissertation on the Sand Creek affair. Other projects followed, but I could not dismiss Slough and Rynerson. I intended to submit the paper for publication, but somehow it seemed incomplete. Questions persisted that I could not answer. The late Robert N. Mullin, to whom this work is dedicated, Joseph W. Snell, the former executive director of the Kansas State Historical Society and an authority on frontier violence, and Robert W. Larson, eminent New Mexico historian and one of the commentators for the 1972 session, provided critical advice on the manuscript. With their suggestions as a base, I persisted in the quest for additional information that might answer the questions that remained. The research was not constant or sustained but rather a kind of persistent interest to which I gave piecemeal and occasional attention over the years.

Not until 1987, fifteen years after I presented the original paper, did I determine to complete the study. The result is this book. Its defects are mine, its insights I owe to a surprisingly diverse group of people. Light T. Cummings, a former colleague and an authority on Spanish America, translated the important New Mexico legislative documents into English for me. Robert Svenningsen of the Denver Federal Records Centers provided useful information from the records of that important repository. J. Richard Salazar, chief of Archival Services at the State Records Center and Archives of New Mexico, located and provided me with critical documents when I had given up hope of finding them. Dr. Myra Ellen Jenkins, the dean of New Mexico's historians and the generous State Historian of New Mexico; Lawrence R. Murphy, the biographer of William F.M. Arny; and C. L. Sonnichsen, the always accommodating champion of "grassroots history," provided crucial insights. Richard Maxwell Brown, whose comments about Slough's death spurred my interest in the subject, has encouraged my quest to understand Western violence through the years.

Brenda Sellers, reference librarian at Abraham Baldwin College, worked endlessly to locate and obtain the critical sources I needed to complete my work. Ann R. Hammons and Sandra Hunt, two of my coworkers, were encouragers who kept me going when my enthusiasm began to flag, not only listening patiently but also providing valuable insights. James A. Burran, historian and academic dean at Abraham Baldwin College and a native of New Mexico; Richard Strickland, the director of the Police Academy on our campus and a scholar whose judgment I have learned to trust; Larry McGruder, a thoughtful associate whose probing questions forced me to think and rethink my conclusions; and Eddie Griggs, a behavioral scientist who helped me deal with the mysteries of sociology and psychology, all read portions of the manuscript and offered helpful criticism.

I am indebted to many thoughtful individuals and organizations, including Hardee Allen of the Diplomatic, Legal and Fiscal Branch of the National Archives; the late Bruce Catton, eminent Civil War historian; Stephany Eger, librarian at the Museum of New Mexico in Santa Fe; Richard N. Ellis, now director of the Southwest Studies Program at Fort Lewis State College, in Durango Colorado; Hazel A. Engel of Willmar, Minnesota; Frances Forman, assistant librarian at the Cincinnati Historical Society; Charles R. Goslin of Lancaster, Ohio; Shirley Hickman of the Manuscripts Department of the Henry E. Huntington Library, San Marino, California; the late William A. Keleher, attorney and New Mexico historian; Susie M. Montoya, District Court clerk, First Judicial District Court at Santa Fe; Dolores G. Martinez, clerk of the District Court, Fourth Judicial District at Las Vegas, New Mexico; James L. Murphy of Ohio State University; Elmer O. Parker, of the Old Army Division, Military Archives Branch, National Archives; G. Martin Ruoss, Special Collections librarian at the Zimmerman Library of the University of New Mexico; Glen S. Slough of Maitland, Florida; M. C. Slough of St. Marys, Kansas; Margaret J. Sparks, research librarian at the Arizona Historical Society; and Jeff Thomas of the Ohio Historical Society.

Finally, Debbie Lawrence, the able secretary of the Social Science Division at Abraham Baldwin College, provided valuable assistance in the preparation of the manuscript.

To all of these people I am grateful. I can only hope that the results will be worthy of their efforts on my behalf.

G.L.R.

Death Comes for the Chief Justice

New Mexico and the Politics of Mistrust

Politics in New Mexico during the Reconstruction following the Civil War reflected a pattern of life peculiar to the region and a variety of interests only faintly connected to national issues. New Mexico was still largely undeveloped and thinly populated, and the Civil War left the territory violent and divided. Its multi-ethnic population surrendered politics to the politicians, in whose hands the larger territorial questions — Indian policy, peonage, the administration of justice, economic growth — were often choked by a miasma of family ties, cultural differences, local interests, and political jobbery. Republicans and Democrats alike protested loyalties to larger principles, but their rhetoric failed to obscure partisan advantage as the fundamental principle. And partisan advantage began in Washington, D.C., where the dominant political party dispensed patronage and government contracts to loyal party members.

Patronage was the key to relations with Washington, and patronage politics issued a set of carpetbaggers and scalawags for New Mexico worthy of the Dunningesque stereotypes who bought gold spitoons in South Carolina and signed liquor bills in Louisiana.[1] The bitter calumny of local politics swallowed up most appointees, no matter how lofty their ideals. Job security depended on a precarious balance between local alliances and loyalty to the national party. The contortions of local politicians produced strange and inconsistent caricatures of real issues: The loudest opponents of slavery were often those who held the most *peons* in serfdom. Democrats and Republicans changed colors in chameleon fashion with the shifting balance of national leadership and local interests. The result was a grotesque parody of responsible government kept in motion by the quest for favors in Washington.

Those who profited most were local *ricos* (wealthy Hispanos), American entrepreneurs, and federal officials, men who shared a common interest in politics as the way to wealth and power. After all, political power was the central issue. Without it, neither the objectives of honorable men nor the material rewards of power could be attained. In this respect New Mexico was not unique. Patronage politics had always been part of the territorial system. The people of the territories, reflecting a growing cynicism about government, expected and accepted the system.[2] At the end of the war, exploitation was virtually a national mood, as much a part of the motivation of the settler as the politician. Yet the Reconstruction's bloody-shirt rhetoric, filled with charges of "Copperheadism" and disloyalty, served to increase suspicions and hatreds in New Mexico beyond the normal name-calling and political in-fighting associated with territorial politics.[3]

At least once during the Reconstruction, the partisan clamor in New Mexico resulted in a tragic and unnecessary death. When William Logan Rynerson, a senator from Dona Ana County, killed John Potts Slough, Chief Justice of the Supreme Court of New Mexico Territory, the violent death of one so prominent at the hands of another public official cast a shadow over the territory and established a reputation for violence and assassination that persists today in histories of New Mexico and studies of American violence.[4] If the preeminent authority on the history of American violence, Richard Maxwell Brown, is correct in his conclusion that New Mexico is "apparently the only place in America where assassination became an integral part of the political system," the Slough-

Rynerson quarrel appears to have been the beginning of a period of officially condoned and/or excused violence.[5] Yet Slough's murder was not the first seed of some malignant force generated by the Civil War, for violence was endemic in New Mexico long before John Slough or William Rynerson arrived in the territory.

New Mexicans had lived in a perpetual state of war since the days of the Spanish Conquest. Unlike Kentucky, where the "dark and bloody ground" of Indian warfare spanned a mere twenty years, or the High Plains, where the struggle lasted thirty, New Mexico experienced more than two centuries of sustained violence. No generation and few families were immune to the sanguinary costs of that bitter inheritance or the hatreds it spawned.[6]

The Indian wars were still very real during the Reconstruction years and would remain a feature of New Mexican life well into the 1880s.[7] This reality seasoned the attitudes of New Mexicans, manifesting as a tight-jawed acceptance of the violence in their midst that spilled over into other relationships — especially when accompanied by institutions such as Indian slavery and peonage and by the attitudes of arrogant Anglo-Americans who far too often added injury to insult in dealing with Hispanos.[8]

Isolation also contributed to New Mexico's heritage of violence. Even during its beginnings as the northern outpost of Spanish civilization in North America, New Mexico received little contact with the centers of political power. The result was an almost feudal relationship between *patrones* and church and *peons* that concentrated real power in the hands of a small number of families and priests. Far from royal authority, the practical political system consisted of a series of local power brokers — alcaldes, prefects, *patrones,* and priests — with a governor to act as final arbiter. Life in New Mexico settled into a kind of eternal present in which the isolated communities lived according to local rules, and order and justice were maintained by local officials who were largely free to act as they chose. Rivalries, family feuds, autocratic practices, and the ever-present threat of Indian attack drove the isolated groups together, created community loyalties, and fostered fear and distrust of outsiders in general and rivals in particular.[9]

Throughout the long history of New Mexico, rebellions and assassinations and political coups were commonplace. Civil and church officials quarreled over jurisdictions from the time the first settlements were planted; during the half-century after 1610 many of the lasting animosities and factions were set in open and often violent conflict. The great rebellion of the Pueblo Indians in 1680 virtually forced the abandonment of New Mexico for a time, and the reconquest in 1693–1694 was brutal and harsh.[10] Mexico declared its independence in 1821, and New Mexico settled into a period of relative calm — until 1837, when the poor of Taos rose up and beheaded Governor Albino Perez and declared one Jose Gonzalez, a buffalo hunter, to be the new governor. Manuel Armijo defeated the rebels the same year, executed Gonzalez, and placed himself in the governorship.[11]

The creation of the Republic of Texas generated more conflict as the expansion-minded *Tejanos* tested the limits of their western border and sought to infringe upon the lucrative Santa Fe trade. The Texan Santa Fe expedition of 1841 heightened tensions and created more violence, resulting in an attempt on the life of the American consul, Manuel Alvarez.[12] Two years later, Texans killed several residents of Mora; in reaction, nativists threatened the lives of American traders. The Texans caused still more grief when Jacob Snivley's expedition murdered a prominent Hispano merchant on the Santa Fe Trail.[13]

In 1846, with the outbreak of the Mexican War, Stephen Watts Kearney invaded the province. Charles Bent, one of the Missouri traders, became the first governor of an American New Mexico.[14] Resentments were great, and early in January 1847, Donaciano Vigil, the territorial secretary, uncovered an anti-American plot to assassinate Bent and others. The ringleaders were exposed, but before the month was out, the Taos Indians mobbed the governor's home; Bent was killed and scalped. The bloody toll ended when U.S. forces under General Sterling Price defeated the rebels. Tomasito, the rebels' leader, was murdered by a guard. Many of the other rebels were tried and hanged.[15] Afterward, New Mexico faced four years of military rule, which generated still more anger and conflict. The dispute between advocates of accommodation and supporters of native home rule dominated the political scene; in the delegate election of 1851 the political rivalry was so intense that William C. Skinner, one of those supporting accommodation, was murdered.[16]

Political turmoil and violence in New Mexico in the nineteenth century owed much to the peculiar configurations of Anglo-American and Mexican-American influences. The same year that Mexico declared independence, the Anglo-American invasion began with the establishment of the Missouri–Santa Fe trade connection. The arrival of the Americans added market capitalism to the political mix. Trade, fur trapping, and land speculation challenged the local economic system and introduced a new and arrogant kind of outside challenge to the New Mexico establishment, and by the time of Kearney's invasion American merchants were a potent force in New Mexico politics.[17]

The problem was not a simple dichotomy between the interests of native New Mexicans, on the one hand, and newcomers, on the other. Rather, the conflict centered on the survival of familial and church politics that dated from the time of Spanish rule, with all of the cultural assumptions about land, people, and law that the traditional order implied, and on efforts to "Americanize" New Mexico by displacing Hispanic tradition and law with Anglo-American law and cultural values.[18]

Hispanos generally resisted the erosion of traditional culture, but their methods varied according to social, economic, and political interests. For *los hombres pobres,* the majority of poor Hispanos, the most common response was evasion: simple avoidance of Anglo influences. They wished only to be left alone. When that proved impossible, they either responded to the leadership of *ricos,* priests, and *jefes politicos,* or resorted to more violent forms of resistance. *Los pobres* provided the manpower for rebellion and social banditry and night riding as well as for electoral majorities.[19]

Most Anglo politicians, however, confined their relations to the *ricos,* clerics, and *jefes politicos,* mostly the heads of New Mexico's great families, who controlled the voters at the local level. These men had strong vested interests in maintaining the traditional system. Some were strongly anti-American and accommodated the invaders reluctantly and only in ways that served their interests, preserving prerogatives, securing land grant titles, and maintaining privileges, custom, and tradition. Others, who recognized a certain inevitability in the Americanization of New Mexico or whose economic interests tied them more directly to Anglo-American business groups, found ways to cooperate.[20]

The complicating factor was that not even the division between those who were patently anti-American and those who were openly accommodationist could be counted on to explain political affiliations, because superimposed over their necessary connections to the Anglos and their vital interests in the government of the territory was a web of family rivalries, church-secular competition, and personal animosities that often dictated strange and tenuous alliances. Consequently, party connections had little meaning in terms of national issues or ideology, and for most of the period prior to

1870, Hispanos regarded themselves as members of the "Chaves Party" or the "Gallegos Party" or the "Perea Party" rather than as Democrats, Whigs, or Republicans.[21]

Anglo-American politics was scarcely more comprehensible. General Kearney and the majority of American merchants in New Mexico worked to impose Anglo-American legal practices, economic assumptions, and cultural values upon the "misguided" and "backward" natives. During the years after 1846, military and commercial interests continued the transformation of New Mexico by placing Anglos in key political posts. Other newcomers, men like James Calhoun and Richard Hanson Weightman, sought to cooperate with the natives and to find an accommodation with them.[22] Others simply realized that the traditional system better served their particular interests.

Anglos were divided over national issues such as slavery and abolition in the 1850s, but the most persistent divisions concerned statehood, the role of the military in civil affairs, Indian policy, and the settlement of land grant disputes, all of which were territorial questions demanding federal involvement. At another level, economic interests clashed. Old established firms were challenged by nascent entrepreneurs. Mining, ranching, land speculation, freighting and railroad schemes all divided the politicos.[23]

During the 1850s most of the appointed federal officers were Anglos, while the legislative assembly was predominantly Hispano. This stalemate made some kind of accommodation essential. Both groups realized that the common key to their multiple interests was influence in Washington. Patronage, more than any other one thing, turned disparate factions into political alliances, and alliances into parties. In practice that meant that virtually all groups came to accept a *modus vivendi* that transposed new governmental forms onto an essentially traditional system. Hence, a legal system resembling those of other American territories and states in

Santa Fe. The southeast corner of the Plaza, showing the Exchange Hotel (La Fonda), at center, and the Seligmann and Clever Store, 1855. *Courtesy of Museum of New Mexico. Neg. no. 10685.*

fact preserved many of New Mexico's old ways. Prefects became probate judges — in time the most powerful local officers in New Mexico — and alcaldes became justices of the peace. These officials, drawn from the same local families that had dominated the communities for years, maintained traditional ways, usurped the legitimate powers of the territorial courts, and dominated elections.[24]

At the heart of the process was a mutually beneficial form of political corruption that allowed seemingly incompatible goals to be achieved by all parties to the system. The bulk of the Hispanic population lived north of Albuquerque and west of the Sangre de Christo Mountains. The Rio Arriba country, as the area was called, was the most heavily populated part of the territory, but it initially offered few attractions to Anglos. The real treasure of Rio Arriba was Hispano votes.

Anglos wanted those votes. *Ricos* and *jefes politicos* controlled them. Unaccustomed to democracy and used to a deferential way of life, *los pobres* were willing to barter their votes in exchange for noninterference with cultural practices, traditions, and the essentials of land and water. The use *patrones* made of the votes did not concern them so long as their way of life remained undisturbed. *Patrones* parleyed their control of the votes into political and economic advantages with the new Anglo system. And Anglos were willing to tolerate — and even encourage — a bastard political system that allowed them to pursue very different goals from the voters who sustained them.

New Mexico politics remained a welter of local interests without a real party system, an effective judiciary, or shared values. Isolation insulated the communities and fostered a paranoia about outsiders. New Mexico politics was interest politics, and partisan advantage was the active ingredient. That reality insured a volatile system marked by intimidation and fraud. Alliances were tenuous at best and sometimes treacherous. Defections and realignments were commonplace simply because the factions lacked substantive links on policy questions. And without real common denominators, the various groups clashed from time to time over the central issues of land, water, patronage, and law.

The peculiar character of politics that was rooted in the cultural differences between Hispanos and Anglos and the *modus vivendi* created to resolve the conflict did not always reveal itself in ways patently ethnic. Rather, the peculiarities tinctured all politics and created a systemic frustration that expressed itself in a general political instability. New Mexicans lived in an atmosphere of suspicion and distrust without shared values.[25] A general lack of confidence in the ability of government officials to govern fairly created the seedbed for violence. The insidious nature of politics created a conspiratorial environment that not only made intrigue the standard for political behavior but also enlarged the potential for violence through the sheer animosity that the system built between individuals.

Then came the Civil War.

CHAPTER 1

The Republican Ascendancy in New Mexico

The political climate that spawned the death of John Potts Slough was a legacy of the Civil War. Of all the Western territories, New Mexico had come closest to secession. At the outset of the war, Southern sentiment was so strong that many observers fully expected the territory to attach itself to the Confederacy. The territory was linked to the South commercially, and territorial officers were mostly Democrats and Southern sympathizers. Southern success appeared to be a *fait accompli* when President Abraham Lincoln appointed Dr. Henry F. Connelly as governor of New Mexico Territory.[1] Connelly was a Democrat, but his devotion to the Union and his influence among the Spanish-speaking natives were unquestioned. Hispanos supported the Union cause virtually without exception, possibly due to their fears of the Texans; with that broad base of support, Connelly rallied Union supporters and managed to return a Unionist majority to the territorial legislature, sending Judge John S. Watts to Washington as territorial delegate. The final blow to secessionist hopes came the following spring, when the Confederate invasion of New Mexico was stalled at the Battle of Glorieta.[2]

Glorieta assured Union control of New Mexico but not political stability. New Mexico had no political parties worthy of the name. The party labels were appropriated by a multiplicity of factions, the real loyalties of which were linked to ethnic, economic, and personal issues at the local level and to the *modus vivendi* worked out in the 1850s. All of the old divisions, suspicions, and interests remained intact, only poorly camouflaged by the all-encompassing blanket of "Union." Apathy was the prevailing attitude toward national issues.[3]

The territory was still plagued with economic problems, including some new ones created by the war. The war intensified the Indian troubles that had been a fundamental reality in New Mexico's life since the days of Spanish conquest. With the withdrawal of regular troops, both the Navajos and the Mescalero Apaches increased their raids on the settlers, killing citizens and imposing a heavy toll in property and livestock. Even so, Indian slavery and peonage still excited concern among Anglo politicians with abolitionist leanings or philanthropic impulses. Education, legal reform, the court system, and statehood also were issues of importance. Yet instead of attacking these issues, politicians — calling themselves Republicans — extolled the policies of the national administration; others, nominally Democrats, sought a low profile under the anonymity of the label Unionist. The real concerns involved local interests.

Early in September 1862, General James Henry Carleton assumed command of the military department of New Mexico. Carleton, a War Democrat with a passionate hatred for the Confederacy, determined to stamp out secessionist sentiment and to bring an end to the Indian wars in New Mexico. Once established at Santa Fe, the general dispatched Colonel Christopher C. "Kit" Carson, New Mexico's most famous Indian fighter, against the Mescalero Apaches and set plans in motion for a reservation at Bosque Redondo on the Pecos River. Carleton planned to concentrate both the Mescaleros and the Navajos there under the supervision of the army while they were taught the "arts of civilization." He saw the Bosque Redondo project as a model for reforming Indian

General James H. Carleton and friends. The distinguished group, representing the Masonic Temple of Santa Fe, taken December 26, 1866, includes several prominent figures in New Mexico politics. Standing left to right are: Col. E. H. Bergman, Charles P. Clever, Col. Nelson H. Davis, Col. Herbert M. Enos, Surgeon Basil K. Norris, and Col. J. C. McFerran. Seated left to right are: Col. D. H. Rucker, Kit Carson, and Brigadier General James H. Carleton. *Photo by Nicholas Brown. Courtesy of Museum of New Mexico. Neg. no. 9826.*

policy on a broader scale. Carson's aggressive campaign against the Apaches forced their surrender, and while they moved onto the new reservation, Carson turned to the far more formidable task of subduing the huge Navajo nation.[4]

General Carleton won initial support for his aggressive Indian policies from nearly everyone, including Bishop Jean B. Lamy (the territory's leading cleric), most politicians, innumerable merchants ambitious for government contracts, and the territory's two leading newspapers. By the summer of

1863, Carleton was the territory's reigning hero. Through liberal use of martial law, he was also the virtual military dictator of New Mexico. No effective voice was yet raised against him, and, so far, the sickly Governor Connelly had cooperated with the general. Nevertheless, politicians and civilian authorities sullenly chafed under Carleton's rule.[5]

Then Carleton's Indian policies began to go sour. The reservation at Bosque Redondo fell victim to a drought and to its antiquated annuity system.[6] With the defeat of the Navajos, the reservation population skyrocketed. Costs also soared. The Apaches and Navajos quarreled with each other incessantly; officials of the Indian bureau quarreled with Carleton's officers. Humanitarians publicly attacked the deplorable conditions on the reservation. Settlers claimed that renegades used the reserve as a base for operations and as a hiding place from retribution. Disappointed contractors charged fraud in awarding contracts.

This was the flaw the politicians needed. William F.M. Arny, the territorial secretary and a man of long experience in political matters, emerged as the leading critic of Carleton's policies. A staunch Republican with practical experience in "Bleeding Kansas," Arny was a recent arrival to the territory who resented the predominantly Democratic clique that ran territorial affairs. Largely through his machinations, James L. Collins, superintendent of Indian Affairs and Carleton's ally, was replaced by Dr. Michael Steck, a kindly man who protested vehemently against Carleton's treatment of the Indians. Now, the disgruntled politicians began to come out of hiding.[7]

Carleton quickly found his policies regarding martial law under attack. The newly bold opposition charged him with subverting the civil liberties of the people and usurping the legitimate power of the courts.[8] The opposition also took advantage of the old anti-military bias among both Hispanics and long-time Anglo residents that dated from the period of military rule following the Mexican War. Around these issues swelled the malcontents, with their own pet schemes for government contracts, development of the Bosque Redondo as a ranching area, organization of a new territory in southern New Mexico, and even restoration of the profits and slaves that had been the by-products of the Indian wars in New Mexico.[9]

By 1864 the territory's leadership was divided into three camps, with Carleton's policies as the fulcrum of controversy. The majority of Republicans, including Connelly, Francisco Perea, and even Kirby Benedict, chief justice of the territorial Supreme Court, initially cooperated with Carleton. They supported President Lincoln, while Arny's group favored the Radicals and openly opposed Carleton. The Democrats, such as they were, actively supported Carleton's policies in New Mexico and George B. McClellan's candidacy for president. Of these groups the Radicals were the most active. Fortunately for them, Connelly's failing health and frequent absences from the territory greatly enhanced Arny's political clout and provided him with a chance to assert his opinions in policy making. This factor precipitated a controversy when Connelly objected to Arny's usurpation of his power. But Arny had ties in Washington, and when he recommended that printing contracts be given to the Santa Fe *New Mexican* (in which Kirby Benedict had an interest) instead of the pro-Carleton Santa Fe *Gazette,* Judge Benedict added his voice to the anti-Carleton forces. This move solidified the Republican coalition under Arny and Benedict against Carleton, who by then had openly endorsed McClellan and the Democrats. However, Carleton retained the support of most of the territorial officers, Democrats, and a few Republican dissidents.[10]

By the end of 1864, Arny was looking beyond Carleton to the organization of a unified Republican party held in line by the dispensation of patronage, grounded on the principle of home rule, and maintained by unswerving support of congressional Radicals. And the plan worked — for a time. Like other New Mexico politicians before him, Arny accepted the *modus vivendi* with Hispanos in matters of local concern. Affiliating himself with such native politicians as Jose Francisco Chaves and the Perea family, Arny accomplished the seemingly impossible. Out of this bitter, emotional, confused, and complicated state of affairs, out of the choking growth of alliances, factions, and illogical connections, the Republican party — or what passed for the Republican party — emerged from the Civil War as the dominant political force in New Mexico.[11]

Led by Arny and Benedict, the Republicans secured a majority in both houses of the legislature and sent Jose Francisco Chaves to Washington as territorial delegate in 1865. Chaves was deeply rooted in New Mexico's past. His grandfather, Don Francisco Chavez, had served as governor of the region when it was part of the Republic of Mexico, and his father, Don Mariano Chavez, had married into the influential Perea family and served under General Manuel Armijo during the revolution of 1837. Don Mariano had read the future clearly and sent his son to St. Louis University to learn English and "come back prepared to defend your people."[12] After completing his university training, the young Chaves attended the College of Physicians and Surgeons at New York City and returned to New Mexico in 1852 with a medical degree and an Anglicized last name.[13]

During the 1850s, Dr. Chaves served in the military campaigns against the Navajos. With the outbreak of the Civil War in 1861, Chaves was commissioned a major in the First New Mexico Infantry. He served with distinction at Valverde, established and commanded Fort Wingate, and left the service in 1865 at the rank of lieutenant-colonel. By then he had also been admitted to the bar. This rather remarkable record of achievement for a man then only thirty-two years old, and his obvious influence with the Hispanic population of the territory, made Chaves almost unbeatable in 1865.[14]

Chaves's broad experience uniquely prepared him for the political arena. He was atypical among New Mexico's native sons, but he was clearly a defender of the old, conservative Mexican-American interests in New Mexico. He lacked Arny's commitment to Republican principles and Benedict's flare for the dramatic. In fact, Chaves differed sharply with the Anglo leadership on most issues. He staunchly defended the old order, including the peonage system, which certainly did not please the anti-slavery Radicals or the business-minded newcomers. These groups, however, had no illusions about his dedication to party principles.

Chaves understood practical politics. His connections to influential groups, especially the powerful Pino family, temporarily outweighed his political inconsistencies. Although ill-informed on such national issues as the Reconstruction, Chaves proved effective as a patronage-broker in Washington. His natural conservatism initially drew him toward the policies of Andrew Johnson, and he became a supporter of Johnsonian Reconstruction. He nurtured a relationship with Johnson that gave him considerable clout in patronage matters. During the early months of Johnson's presidency, this posed no serious problem for New Mexico's Radicals; indeed, for the moment Republicans of all stripes enjoyed their domination of New Mexico politics with a show of unanimity.[15]

Even the Republicans' impressive margin of control was subject to the fiat of Washington's patronage-mongers, however, and the remnants of General Carleton's Union party stood poised to jerk power from Republican hands at the slightest mistake.[16] No one understood the fragile nature of the Republican hold on New Mexico better than Arny, and when rumors reached New Mexico that changes were contemplated in the territorial offices, even he confessed that it would be advantageous "to *ignore* all applications from persons in New Mexico *and appoint well known and reliable*

Republicans who have never been here."[17] Lincoln had made
no changes, but Johnson's independent course heightened
Republican fears, and in February 1866, Johnson announced
that Arny, Benedict, and Connelly would be replaced.[18] Republican unity would now be tested.

The Republicans of New Mexico had good reason to be
apprehensive about the men appointed to replace Connelly,
Arny, and Benedict. The new appointees were conservatives
of Democratic extraction, but they came to the territory with
the blessing of Delegate Chaves, who remained close to the
President and more than a little conservative himself. Robert
Byington Mitchell, a Civil War general who had served in
Nebraska and Wyoming against the warring tribes of the
Central Plains in 1864 and 1865, was appointed governor,
and John P. Slough, another unemployed Union general,
succeeded Benedict as chief justice. These appointments
jeopardized Republican gains and threatened Chaves's connection to Radical Republicans in New Mexico. In the building fight between Congress and the President, New
Mexicans were too visibly connected to Johnson. With the
elections of 1866, shrewd politicians realized that a major
confrontation was brewing; with Arny soon to be out of office,
the Radicals knew they were in danger of losing their powerful position.

Their fears were soon justified. "Bobby" Mitchell was
quickly drawn into the web of factionalism. James L. Collins,
former superintendent of Indian Affairs and the federal depositor; John T. Russell, Collins's partner and editor of the
Santa Fe *Gazette;* Attorney General Charles P. Clever, and
other former Democrats and pro-Carleton Republicans cultivated Mitchell's friendship, and given Mitchell's conservative
proclivities, he naturally was attracted to them more than to
Arny's Radical Republicans, who soon came to despise Mitchell as an overbearing, intolerant, and thoroughly unaccept-
able governor.[19]

Robert Byington Mitchell, governor of New Mexico Territory, 1866–1869. *Courtesy of Kansas State Historical Society, Topeka.*

John P. Slough fared better. He was, after all, a hero of special importance to New Mexico. He had commanded the Union troops at Glorieta in 1862, when the Confederate advance into New Mexico was stalled and the West was saved for the Union. That, along with a reputation for honesty, gallantry, and judicial experience, gave him widespread support. But John Slough shared with Robert Mitchell a short temper and an outspoken opinion. For all of his integrity and good intentions, he possessed a violent disposition that often exploded in an effusion of coarse and profane language. Slough had an exaggerated sense of personal honor that caused him to view the slightest criticism as insult. Stubbornness and dogmatism compounded the problem of excitability. These qualities were to determine his fate in New Mexico.

Slough was born in Cincinnati, Ohio, on February 1, 1829. He became a lawyer in his home state and was elected to the state legislature when he was twenty-one years old. Slough rose rapidly in the Democratic party, and by 1856 he was considered a party leader. In that presidential election year, he served as secretary of the Democratic State Central Committee. He conducted himself well and managed to get reelected to the legislature from Hamilton County. At the time, Slough was described as "decidedly a fine looking man, tall and well built, with light hair and complexion, round face, and head approaching the Shakespearean form." He was said to handle himself well in the legislature, "with the great propriety of not mixing too much in discussion." He was "quite the gentleman, social, free and sufficiently dignified."[20]

But the "gallant but bellicose" Slough soon won a reputation as a quarrelsome and pugnacious adversary. Late in 1856, he knocked down and then pummeled a Republican named Baker in an altercation that soon had the Democratic journals chortling while Republicans raged. Then on the morning of January 14, 1857, Slough introduced a measure of small importance concerning travel expenses of legislators. In a private aside to Slough, Darius Cadwell, the representative from Ashtabula, opined that the matter was "too foolish and frivolous" for the attorney general's attention. An argument ensued. Slough swore that he would not be called a fool; Cadwell demanded to know what Slough proposed to do about it, whereupon Slough struck Cadwell in the forehead with his fist.

The incident was over so quickly that few representatives were even aware that it had occurred. But Cadwell marched to the front of the chamber and dramatically demanded Slough's apology. Flustered and angry, Slough refused, instead demanding that a committee investigate the incident. His angry performance proved to be a critical error in judgment that he did not seek to correct even after he had time to reflect on his actions. Two days later, Slough read a statement to the legislature in which he expressed regret that the incident had occurred on the floor of the House but insisted that the offense had merited the punishment, declaring that any future attack to his honor would produce the same response.[21]

This unrepentant spirit provoked an instantaneous reaction in the Republican press. Not only did the Republican editors deplore Slough's attitude and compare him to Preston Brooks, who had only months before beaten Senator Charles Sumner on the floor of the Senate, but they also implored him to end the farce by admitting his error. On January 24, Slough defiantly declared that he had made all the apology he intended to make. Afterward, a resolution was introduced demanding that Slough extend "a full and unequivocal confession, without reserve, of the wrong done, with an assurance that it shall not be repeated." If Slough refused, the resolution insisted, he would be expelled.[22] The measure, however, did not pass, and for the next week the House wrangled over what should be done. On the final day of debate, William M. Corry, a Democratic representative from Slough's home county who had not been present when the original incident occurred, unleashed a surprisingly harsh attack on his colleague. At one point, Slough called Corry to order, swearing to hold Corry accountable for what he had said. Corry retorted, "And I will be prepared for you, here and elsewhere." He then proceeded to lecture the Democrats for supporting Slough. Later another delegate made a speech so bitter that even a Republican correspondent described it as "a very bad harangue, so far forgetting himself at one time as to apply epithets to Mr. Slough, whose scourged spirit he was so awkwardly picking."[23] During that speech, Slough grew so angry that he exclaimed he would not stand for the abuse any longer and had to be literally held in his chair by friends. Outside the legislature, his remarks were so intemperate that even his allies were embarrassed. When the ordeal finally ended, Slough was expelled from the House by a vote of seventy-one to thirty-three.[24]

Slough's expulsion did not end the affair. A special election was called to fill his seat, and Slough sought vindication from his constituents. In a bitterly partisan fight, Slough's conduct was dissected by the press, while the Democrats unleashed a firestorm of criticism against Corry for his attack on Slough. When the election was finally held on February 16, 1857, virtually everyone breathed a sigh of relief, but even then an apparent Slough victory was overturned when an error was found in the vote count. Although he considered challenging the reversal, Slough accepted defeat, and the farce came to an end.[25]

It had been an astonishing affair, most particularly because everyone concerned, Republicans and Democrats alike, agreed that if Slough had simply apologized in full, the whole episode would have been avoided. Correspondents admitted that Slough's act was "not the act of cowardly premeditation, but of momentary impulse and excitement."[26] What puzzled everyone was his refusal to admit his mistake. One representative wrote that "if Mr. Slough, after committing the assault had, when sufficient time had elapsed for his blood to cool, shown that he did not approve of personal violence, except in self-defense, on the floor of a legislative body; that his judgment disapproved his act, the result would have been far different."[27] The Cincinatti *Gazette* agreed, suggesting that if Slough had apologized, "he would have been passed over with a resolution of censure, and perhaps even that would not have been adopted."[28] William Corry was more direct: "We could sit with a savage who repented and asked forgiveness, but not with one who persisted in the injury, and constantly, by speech and writing, threatened its repetition."[29] The episode revealed the personality flaws that would attend John Slough throughout his career.

Ohio pundits pronounced Slough politically dead, but he continued to speak out on public questions. He lectured on the troubles in Kansas, and in 1858 he decided to try his fortunes there. He was soon inmeshed in that territory's explosive politics and for a time seemed a possible choice for governor. But in Kansas, too, Slough's temper precipitated controversy and thwarted his ambitions. In November 1859, the Cleveland *Leader* reported that Slough, who left Ohio democracy for "the more congenial company of border ruffians," was on the Kansas state ticket as lieutenant governor. Said the editor, "No marvel they put him on the Democratic ticket." By year's end, with his political prospects gloomy in Kansas, Slough joined the Pike's Peak gold rush and was chosen as the "Sole Judge of the Appellate Court under the People's Government of Colorado Territory" by the miners.[30]

In 1861, Governor William Gilpin appointed Slough commander of the First Colorado Volunteer Regiment, primarily on the strength of Slough's recruiting efforts and his reputation for courage and determination. He was not, however, a popular choice. One of his soldiers said of him:

He has a noble appearance, but the men seem to lack
confidence in him. Why, I cannot say — nor can they, I
think. His aristocratic style savors more of eastern society
than of the free-and-easy border to which he should have
become acclimated, but that it is bred in the bone.[31]

Slough's quarrelsome nature reasserted itself in conflicts
with his staff officers, especially with Samuel F. Tappan, his
second officer in command, and the Reverend John M.
Chivington, the volatile and ambitious regimental major —
both men with no mean reputations as storm centers. These
rivalries so seriously undermined the efficiency of Slough's
regiment that only fortunate accidents prevented the battle
of Glorieta from becoming a Union debacle.[32]

Slough marched to meet the Confederates in direct defiance of orders, with a command so seriously divided that he
feared for his own safety. He always believed that attempts
were made on his life on two different occasions during the
campaign. Indeed, Slough was so convinced that some officers and enlisted men of the regiment planned to assassinate
him that he resigned his commission on the heels of the
Glorieta victory.[33] Reminiscences of soldiers who served
under him in the New Mexico campaign indicate that Slough
was "a man of undoubted ability and bravery, but his personal contact with men was never of a kind to make him
beloved. He wanted tact and policy."[34]

After Glorieta, Slough departed for the East with the
blessing of Colorado's Governor Gilpin. A brigadier's stars
were to be given to a Coloradan, and Slough won them in
spite of the best efforts of Major Chivington's friends to secure them for the "Fighting Parson."[35] In August 1862,
Slough was assigned as military governor at Alexandria, Virginia, a post he held until the end of the war. Although a
Democrat, John Slough moved in the right circles in Wash-

ington. Despite his pre-war position on Kansas, he was a favorite of Edwin McMasters Stanton, who used Slough frequently for court martial duty, including such important cases as the trial of General Fitz-John Porter.[36] He was on hand to apply pressure at the War Department when Colorado officers protested against the Sand Creek Massacre, which had been led by Slough's old nemesis, John Chivington.[37] He served as a pallbearer at President Lincoln's funeral and as a bodyguard for President Johnson.[38]

But the Washington years were not without difficulties. In June 1863, Slough became embroiled in a quarrel with General Joseph Hooker that almost resulted in his arrest for obstruction of orders. He was saved in that instance only because General Hooker himself was removed from command.[39] Slough possessed a remarkable repertory of profanity that, when added to his fiery temper, usually resulted in a most colorful repartee. In May 1863, a citizen of Alexandria charged Slough with "language unbecoming an officer and a gentleman." The aggrieved businessman accused Slough of calling him "a God damned scoundrel . . . together with other opprobrious epithets." He also charged that two of Slough's officers had "violently beaten" him "about the head with a loaded whip" with the full approval of General Slough.[40] This incident contributed to Slough's decision to resign his commission; in typical style, even that was attended by an angry letter explaining that the resignation came because President Johnson had "set aside" certain important policies.[41]

By this time Slough was working actively to secure the removal of John Evans, governor of Colorado, in the wake of the investigations into the Sand Creek affair. As early as June 1865, rumors circulated that Slough would succeed Evans.[42] Slough did journey west that summer to his old haunts, but August found him back in Washington and still unemployed. His outspoken criticism of Evans compelled him to withdraw his own name from consideration as governor of

Colorado and left him without any real political prospects.[43]
It was a characteristic move for a man who was often forced
to defend his integrity because of an angry temperament. He
languished in Washington for a time, looking for a position,
and he was still unemployed when President Johnson named
him chief justice of New Mexico's courts in March 1866.[44] "In
view of my military service in New Mexico," Slough confidently predicted, "my appointment as Chief Justice of that
Territory would be acceptable to its people."[45]

Slough arrived in New Mexico with rumors flying about
the possibility of a major Indian war. He promptly offered his
services to the government "in a military capacity." He proposed to raise a regiment of Indian fighters, assuring Secretary of War Stanton that "The men of Colorado and New
Mexico . . . will enlist in the Regular Army under me, if I
should be commissioned therein."[46] When Stanton failed to
respond enthusiastically, Slough accepted his fate and
turned his inexhaustible confidence and energy to other
matters. The brash chief justice became an active promoter
of New Mexico's interests and involved himself in a variety
of projects.[47]

On the bench, Slough proved to be a good trial judge. He
worked hard at his job, and as events turned out, he had
plenty of hard work to do. Courtroom procedures in New
Mexico were extremely lax. The jury system was but a carica-
ture. Juries were frankly partisan, and rules governing the
selection of jurors were largely ignored. The problem was
partially cultural. The *modus vivendi* worked out in the early
years of the territory was especially evident in the courts.
Probate judges — the most powerful local officials in New
Mexico — and justices of the peace acted as prefects and
alcaldes, respectively. In practice, these local officials
usurped the legitimate power of territorial courts and dominated elections.[48] The politicians encouraged many of the bad
practices and used them to partisan advantage within the

many family fiefdoms. Slough was determined to remedy these abuses. Moreover, the new judge worked well with the army, a circumstance of particular significance in light of the stormy history of civil-military relations during Kirby Benedict's tenure as chief justice.[49] In all of this, John Slough was open, honest, and blunt.

For some citizens, Slough's methods were a welcome change. He was not a Republican's man as Benedict had been, and so far he was not the toady of Charles Clever — Carleton's heir apparent — as both of Slough's associates on the bench, Sydney A. Hubbell and Joab Houghton, were alleged to be.[50] Although Slough was a Democrat, he was not yet a partisan in New Mexico's political wars. Still, even attempting to administer justice fairly threatened practices long accepted in New Mexico. More importantly, Slough's course of action placed him unwittingly in league with the "Americanizers" and set him in opposition with the now-venerable *modus vivendi*. From his first days on the bench, Slough experienced bitter feelings against him from some New Mexican politicians, but realization that Slough was being dragged into the political arena didn't occur until the summer of 1866, when Slough joined other Democrats in a memorial supporting Andrew Johnson's efforts *"to stay the threatening tide of RADICALISM."*[51] Some Republicans condemned the memorial as partisan, but even William Arny confessed that "Four-fifths of the voters in this territory are in favor of the President's policy of Reconstruction."[52]

Nevertheless, the Santa Fe *New Mexican* warned of a conspiracy of newcomers who despised the natives to abolish the largely Hispanic legislature and establish government by the governor and the judges.[53] When this far-fetched plot failed to materialize, the Chaves faction chose to avoid pressing the issue of Slough's politics. After all, they could produce no evidence that Slough was deliberately against them or that he desired any overtly political role beyond his legitimate activities as a judge. Still, he was a man who bore watching. What he had done so far could be written off as ignorance, but if he continued, action might have to be taken.

As 1866 waned, the political climate in New Mexico grew deceptively calm. On the surface, the politicos appeared to have reached terms of accommodation at long last. Perhaps they would finally get down to the real needs of the territory. Already, Governor Mitchell could claim some progress for his administration, and the courts were facing some hard questions affecting civil liberties and the future of New Mexico.[54] Mitchell was so pleased with the state of affairs that he decided to leave the territory for the East in order to promote New Mexico mining interests.

Mitchell's departure created a vacuum of sorts, but only for a moment. The territorial secretary ordinarily assumed the role of acting governor during a governor's absence, so Arny stepped into the office and initiated a vigorous, partisan effort on behalf of Republican interests. By the time the legislature met in December 1866, Arny had already appointed a number of officials, awarded printing contracts, and signed official commissions. He even delivered an annual message to the legislature.

These actions went far beyond the normal exercise of administrative duties undertaken by acting governors, and Arny's assumption of so much authority provoked an immediate protest from his opponents, who reminded him that he had been relieved as territorial secretary more than eight months earlier. Arny insisted that his tenure would expire when the new appointee arrived and not until then. For a brief period, the legislature was immobilized by "a state bordering on anarchy," but the Republican majority rallied to Arny's defense and voted into law a package of Arny-sponsored measures.[55]

When Mitchell finally returned to New Mexico in March 1867, the Republicans were entrenched in a strong position.

Throwing caution to the wind, the intemperate governor "stirred up his own storm" when he directly challenged the legality of Arny's conduct. Using arguments marshaled by Charles P. Clever, the attorney general of the territory, Mitchell declared Arny's actions null and void and his appointments invalid. Mitchell even insisted on his right to veto acts that the legislature had passed during his absence. Then he dismissed Arny's appointees and substituted his own slate of territorial officers. Arny turned to Washington for support, and on March 26, 1867, the Congress of the United States passed a memorial supporting Arny's course of action. Even so, Mitchell and Clever kept the dispute alive.[56] Arny's provocative partisanship and Mitchell's high-handed reaction deepened political animosities, and hopes for cooperation withered in the face of continuing controversy.

George R. Estes, Arny's replacement, had yet made no effort to assume the post of territorial secretary. His procrastination prompted Chaves to seek another appointment, and Chaves threw his weight behind the ambitions of Herman H. Heath, another veteran of the Indian campaigns on the plains in 1864 and 1865. Heath was an opportunist whose political principles were pliable at best. A perpetual office-seeker, Heath had been a Democrat before the war. In 1850, he published a newspaper in Washington, D.C., called the *Southern Press,* which advocated the cause of Southern rights. Later, during the Kansas troubles, Heath published a newspaper in Iowa called *The Northwest,* which took a pro-slavery stance. President Buchanan appointed him to be postmaster at Dubuque; he held the post until Lincoln was elected. Then he was replaced "as one of the first sacrifices to Republicanism," as he himself put it.[57]

In 1861, Heath offered his services to the new Confederacy and pledged his undying loyalty to the Southern cause. But when he received no encouragement from the South, he enlisted as a private in Company G of the First Iowa Cavalry at Dubuque. He was so active in recruiting that he was soon commissioned a first lieutenant and regimental adjutant. He was promoted to captain only three months later and assumed command of Company L. His regiment saw service in Missouri against guerrillas, and he acted as provost marshal at Clinton, Missouri. At the Battle of Clear Creek near Springfield, in August 1862, Confederate rifle fire shattered his right elbow, wounded him in the hip, and killed his horse. He lost the use of his right arm and returned home to Dubuque to recover. For several months he was reported absent without leave, but in November 1862 he turned up on General Samuel Ryan Curtis's staff at St. Louis.[58]

Heath was mustered out of service on February 28, 1863, so that he could accept a commission as a major in the Seventh Iowa Cavalry. He was appointed assistant provost marshal for the District of Missouri. Later, he served as chief of cavalry for the District of Nebraska and, briefly, as commanding officer at Fort Kearny on the Overland Trail. Afterward, he rejoined the staff of General Curtis as provost marshal general for the Department of Kansas. Ironically, he was attached to the staff of General Robert Byington Mitchell as chief of cavalry and inspector general early in 1865 and served the remainder of the war on the Platte route searching for Indians. On May 29, 1865, he was mustered out again to accept a commission from the governor of Iowa — as a colonel in the same regiment he formerly had served. In August 1865, Heath was brevetted a brigadier general, retroactively effective from March 13, 1865, for gallant and meritorious services — largely through the efforts of his "very giddy wife," who apparently had connections to Senator Lane of Kansas, or so Heath's enemies attested.[59]

Few people liked H. H. Heath. Captain Eugene F. Ware, who served under him, recalled that most of Heath's officers believed that he was "thoroughly 'secesh,' although professing quite the opposite." Ware described him as "a fine-looking, dressy, showy fellow, but a great scoundrel." He also called Heath "a self-important, dictatorial wind-bag" who "was willing to be a traitor to his country or do anything else. He was absolutely without principle." Heath was dishonorably discharged in May 1866 under questionable circumstances, with unanswered charges about the unauthorized sale of army horses hanging over his head. A week later, the dismissal was suspended until Heath could answer the charges, and he was ordered to appear in Washington. There he managed to defend himself successfully. Ware claimed that Heath's wife personally called on President Johnson "in a beautiful blue moire antique dress . . . and had his dismissal remitted to a discharge from the service."[60]

By then, Heath had already plunged into the politics of Nebraska Territory, setting himself against Nebraska's Republican establishment, which was decidedly Radical in its leanings, and making an open bid for support from President Johnson. As editor of the Nebraska *Republican* and an assiduous letter writer, Heath forced himself into a leadership role with the small conservative faction within the territory's Republican party. Even the conservatives distrusted him, however. He tried to put together a coalition of conservative Republicans and Democrats, but rival patronage goals made agreement between the two groups virtually impossible. He hoped to win the governorship of Nebraska, but reports that Heath was "an adventurer attaching himself to the side that pays best" hurt him in Washington. Eventually, his shady reputation and the lack of support for him in the territory prevented his appointment.[61]

Johnson was also skeptical of Heath's loyalties and alert to the political realities in Nebraska, but his decision left him with one more enemy. Heath was jobless and bitter but subdued his feelings while he waited for another opportunity. It came in New Mexico. Why Jose Francisco Chaves was attracted to such a patently opportunistic man as Heath was never clear, but with Chaves's blessing, Johnson appointed Heath territorial secretary. The appointment pleased Nebraskans of all persuasions and allowed President Johnson to dispose of a troublesome problem. Chaves, however, appeared delighted — describing Heath as "a gentleman of undoubted capacity and sterling integrity" — and openly predicted that Heath would prove to be an invaluable asset to New Mexico Republicans.[62] As an added bonus, on June 22, 1867, Heath was brevetted a major general for his service "against hostile Indians" dating from March 13, 1865.[63]

Ironically, it was the Santa Fe *Gazette* that first applauded Heath's coming, praising Johnson for the appointment of the first "gentleman" to hold the office in years. Upon seeing the item, a Kansas editor declared, "Heath should instantly order a thousand copies of the *Gazette* containing the above, as it is the first time within our knowledge that he has been spoken well of by the press anywhere. The *Gazette* however has this excuse — Heath is as yet a stranger down there."[64]

Not until July 1867, did the new secretary arrive in New Mexico. By then, Chaves was embroiled in an election campaign against Charles Clever, who had challenged him for the delegate seat. Heath immediately joined the fray in behalf of Chaves, but a remarkable metamorphosis had already taken place. The new Heath took the Radical position, urging Republicans to join the Grand Army of the Republic and the Union League and launching a bitter attack on the Democratic party as the party of disloyalty.[65] Heath's aggressive stand for Radical goals reflected the shifting balance in Washington and suggested that both he and Chaves were reading the political signs in Washington very carefully. Heath's conversion was hardly the result of principle. Nevertheless, he went to work at once, throwing all of his energies into building a disciplined party organization in New Mexico. That meant appeasing the Arny group and building ties to Republican Radicals in Washington. The patronage wars were entering a new phase, but Republican solidarity had held.

CHAPTER 2

The Zealot and the Politicos

John Slough did not play a major role in the partisan struggles of 1866 and early 1867. He seemed completely oblivious to the controversy. Even so, friction did build between him and some of the Republican leaders. His abrasive personality was partly responsible. Plainly, John Slough was a difficult man to like. He personalized every criticism, however slight. The most inconsequential affront could set off his hair-trigger temper, and although his anger usually subsided as quickly as it arose, he frequently found himself apologizing for abusive and profane language. Even that was difficult for him. He simply could not admit mistakes because doing so meant a loss of face that his sense of honor would not tolerate. His bulldog refusal to let issues die, even when he was at fault, occasionally bordered on the irrational. His behavior at such moments was simply obnoxious. Slough was a capable man who meant well, but his uncontrollable emotions were not calculated to win him friends.

Still, temper alone was not enough to explain the deliberately provocative attitude that some officials took toward him. Ironically, Slough's greatest weakness was his refusal to be drawn into the political fray. So far, he had maintained a fiercely independent course, ignoring the political clamor and concentrating on his court reforms. But that same independence made him vulnerable. If it gave Slough no enemies, it also left him without firm friends and allies. More importantly, his independence potentially threatened practices and conditions that were critical to the Republican coalition. Clearly, the Republicans distrusted him: in time, they planned to provoke Slough in order to secure an excuse for having him removed. Slough was not their enemy, but he was not their ally, either. The safest course was to replace him with one of their own.

One of Slough's pet projects was the erection of a monument to honor New Mexico's Union dead. Late in 1866, he managed to have a bill introduced in the legislature to authorize the needed monies. The bill created a committee consisting of the chief justice, the territorial secretary, and the territorial treasurer. The bill seemed uncontroversial, but the measure came while Arny was flexing his political muscles. He stepped into the situation and almost precipitated a brawl.

"I suggested to some of the members of the Council that it was discourteous to the Governor to place in the hands of the Chief Justice that which legitimately belonged to the Governor, "Arny explained to Governor Mitchell. "The result was that the Council amended the Law, and Judge Slough in the street denounced all parties interested in language unbecoming a Judge or a gentleman."[1] Arny's concern for a governor he detested was touching — and unconvincing — but the incident emphasized the extent to which politics intruded on even the most nonpartisan issues. For the moment, however, Arny received little more than a tongue-lashing for his trouble.

Slough, for his part, had found an outlet for his insatiable energy in the court system itself. Reforming the jury system almost became an obsession, and Slough was indefatigable in that role. He dismissed juries without pay, imprisoned and fined jurors for misconduct, demanded adherence to the law from sheriffs and their deputies, set aside verdicts, and desperately tried to eliminate politics from the courts. Slough was tampering with some of New Mexico's sacred cows, a

Santa Fe Plaza. East Side, ca. 1868–1869. At left is the monument to the Union dead that Judge Slough worked to build and that provoked a quarrel between him and William Arny. *Courtesy of Museum of New Mexico. Neg. no. 11252.*

practice that won him few friends among the politicians and the power brokers — whatever their political persuasions.

In February 1867, he struck a major blow against peonage in New Mexico in a decision that affected many prominent New Mexican politicians, including Jose Francisco Chaves.[2] Peonage, one of New Mexico's worst cultural practices, began as voluntary servitude to satisfy debts or other obligations. As time passed, however, the concept was extended to include Indian slavery. Routinely, New Mexicans raided Indian villages and made slaves of Indian women and children. Most of the Anglos who moved into New Mexico were appalled by the practice, and from the days of James Calhoun, the early U.S. governor of New Mexico, peonage was routinely denounced. But the practice continued. In 1862, Arny, revealing his strong abolitionist sentiments, attempted to eliminate both Indian slavery and indentured servitude. The legislature refused to act on the matter. Three years later, President Johnson issued a proclamation declaring Indian slavery to be illegal and demanding an immediate end to the practice. Even the passage of the Thirteenth Amendment to the Constitution failed to make a difference.[0]

The reason was simple enough. Indian slavery and peonage were well-established traditions in New Mexico that had the support of the local power elite. The powerful Mexican-American families refused to acquiesce, and they dominated the local politics of New Mexico, much to the chagrin of federal appointees. General Carleton viewed Indian slavery as an effective punishment for hostile Indians. Others argued that ending the system would actually injure the peons. Perhaps most importantly, many Anglos enjoyed the benefits of the system. Even Governor Connelly had used Indian slaves when he was governor. Jose Francisco Chaves stoutly defended the practice in Washington after Senator Charles Sumner introduced legislation specifically designed to end it.[4]

In 1866, local authorities arrested an escaped *peon* named Thomas Heredia and returned him to his "master," Jose Maria Garcia. The justice of the peace in Dona Ana County declared that Heredia's peonage contract was binding. In January 1867, the Heredia case came before the New Mexico territorial Supreme Court. The judges ruled unanimously that New Mexico's peonage law was unconstitutional. Speaking for the court, Judge Slough stated that the law itself established the involuntary character of the servitude in question and bore a strong resemblance to Southern slave codes.[5]

Heredia was set free, but that did not end the controversy. Slough then appointed Samuel Ellison and F. D. Thompson to enforce the edict. Both men traveled throughout the territory, zealously attempting to eradicate peonage, but their successes were limited. In March, Congress passed Sumner's bill, and Governor Mitchell issued a proclamation declaring all New Mexico law at variance with federal statutes to be null and void. And still the practice continued. Even after the army stepped in to enforce federal law, this cultural anachronism lingered in many remote parts of the territory.[6]

In fact, most of the resistance to change had come from men calling themselves Democrats. Even Governor Mitchell was reluctant to act against the system, and the Santa Fe *Gazette* accepted the changes only after the passage of the federal law. Yet, the unanimous decision in the Heredia case was rendered by judges later accused of being Democratic partisans. The fight against peonage had been led by the old Radical war horse, Arny. Stephen B. Elkins, the young acting district attorney, was a zealot on the subject, and Commissioner Ellison was an active Republican.[7] But the movement against peonage was potentially damaging to the party Arny had worked so hard to build. Hispano leaders were not happy with the result. Slough had intruded into territory that affected the interests of Chaves and other Mexican-American *ricos*. His conduct, then, threatened not the ideals of Republican leaders but the practical realities of the Republican coalition. Nothing so graphically demonstrated the peculiar nature of politics in New Mexico as the peonage question.

Slough apparently gave no more thought to the political repercussions of the decision against peonage. He was preoccupied with other matters, including serious financial troubles that winter and spring. In May 1867, Slough arranged a leave of absence to sell properties in Denver, but he was forced to postpone his departure in order to hold court in Albuquerque after Justice Hubbell injured himself in an accident. Slough accepted the chore grudgingly, and he ran the session with a high hand, alienating attorneys and frightening jurors with his behavior.[8]

Among the cases Slough heard was a murder case against Benjamin and William Kelsey and James A. Jeremiah. The Grand Jury returned true bills in the case, but upon Slough's instructions, the case was dropped. A lesser charge, "carrying arms," was subsequently filed against William Kelsey. The prisoner pleaded guilty and was fined fifty dollars. Kelsey's attorneys, W. H. Henrie and Van C. Smith "acknowledged Kelsey's indebtedness to the Territory," but a fifty-dollar fine for carrying arms in a territory where every male in long pants carried a weapon shocked many people. Both Henrie and Smith privately complained about the ruling, and District Attorney Elkins told the judge plainly that jurors were scared of him to the point that verdicts were affected.[9]

When the session ended, Slough made a quick trip to Denver to salvage his finances, but he arrived just as the city was reacting to rumors of a new Indian war. He wrote bitterly to Santiago Hubbell, the brother of Judge Hubbell, "I was unable to sell. The Indian war has so prostrated everything that I failed in the purpose for which I went. . . . Two weeks before I went there I could have received my own prices as the Indian war had not then . . . begun. My going to hold your brothers [*sic*] Courts in Albuquerque has caused me serious inconvenience and much expense."[10]

Judge Slough returned to Santa Fe in time for the July term of the First District Court. It proved to be an exhausting session. Most of the 250 cases he heard were routine matters involving violations of the revenue laws, but several cases were particularly significant. For example, the case of the *United States vs. Guadalupe Mares* reflected a new spirit of cooperation between military and civil authorities in bringing Mares to trial on a charge of selling liquor to Indians. But the jury in the case became hopelessly deadlocked, whereupon Slough dismissed the jury *without pay*. A second panel of jurors was also unable to agree upon a verdict, and its members were discharged *without pay*. Curiously, at that point Mares pleaded guilty, and Slough, who had promised to be lenient, sentenced him to one year in prison.[11] The *New Mexican* applauded the conviction with the observation that "the selling of liquor to Indians has been the cause of great trouble in the Territory, and to this illegal traffic the cause of many of our Indian difficulties can be traced." The paper even gave "great credit" to the military authorities for their role in the case.[12]

Another major decision provoked an entirely different reaction. Stephen B. Elkins, the U.S. Attorney, had worked hard to secure indictments against Comancheros (renegade white and mixed-blood outlaws) who were trading with the Indians for stolen cattle.[13] The government's case rested upon the assertion that the Comancheros were operating in Indian country without proper licenses. Slough quashed the charges, maintaining that there was no "Indian country" in New Mexico within the meaning of the law.[14] Slough was wrong. The Indian Appropriations Act of February 27, 1851, plainly extended federal jurisdiction to New Mexico, and Elkins protested angrily to Washington that the trade with the Comancheros was encouraging the Indians "to kill and rob a portion of our citizens in order to carry on trade with another portion."[15] Henry Stanbery, the attorney general of the United States, instructed Elkins to appeal the decision. Eventually, the New Mexico Supreme Court overruled Slough, but not before Slough was accused of conspiring with desperadoes.[16]

In another important decision, Slough declared the Pueblo Indians to be citizens of the United States.[17] This action was later upheld by the United States Supreme Court. At the time, the decision seemed farsighted, but it greatly complicated Pueblo relations with the United States in the years that followed and did irreparable damage to Pueblo interests.

These decisions caused wide discussion and later provided the basis for an assault on the chief justice's character and judicial conduct. At the time, however, even the Republican-dominated *New Mexican* declared that "great credit is due to John P. Slough for the manner in which he dispatches business and for the firmness and fairness of his decisions."[18]

In August 1867, Slough was in San Miguel County. Encouraged by the favorable response to his reforms, Slough continued his crusade. On August 20, the case of Juan Jose Herrera for "carrying arms" went to a jury, which returned a verdict of guilty. A routine case suddenly produced excitement when Slough learned that Serafin Baca, a young deputy sheriff, had permitted one juror to leave the jury room for half an hour and had delivered a message to another juror. Slough was furious. He sentenced Baca to thirty days in jail for contempt of court. The eighteen-year-old deputy broke down and wept, and local citizens threatened to call a protest meeting, but Elkins and Benedict persuaded the citizens to let the matter pass.

Slough never wavered. He turned his wrath on the wayward jurors. Pedro A. Archuleta and Jose Duran were cited for contempt for "violating their oaths as jurors." That was not the end of the incident. Slough dismissed six jurors without pay and barred them from further service as jurors. Judge Slough then set aside convictions in the cases against Herrera and William Kelsey, the same man who had been before Slough in Bernalillo County the previous May.[19] By the time the rape case of Jesus Truncosa was called, the situation was so tense that Elkins delivered a very long and detailed summation for the jury. When the jury retired to deliberate its verdict, Slough called Elkins aside to ask why Elkins had spoken at such length. Elkins told the judge that the jurors were afraid of Slough and that he feared they would return a guilty verdict regardless of his client's guilt. The jury found Truncosa guilty. When the Grand Jury failed to find an indictment against Juan Leiba in a rape case, Slough remanded the accused to jail and told the sheriff that if he did not keep Leiba there, Slough would have the sheriff arrested and incarcerated at Santa Fe.[20]

In Mora County, Slough permanently struck Cruz Martinez from the Grand Jury rolls and sentenced him to thirty days in jail for contempt when he lied about having served as a grand juror in the March 1866 term of court. When an exuberant Republican named Trinidad Lopez suddenly shouted, "Hurrah for Chaves!" in Slough's court, the judge jailed him for contempt. Lopez escaped that night, only to be caught and hauled back before the judge — who set bail at $1,000 and ordered his case continued to the next term of court.[21] In Santa Ana County Slough was equally stern. Anastacio Garcia, president of the Grand Jury, was "discharged dishonorably" because of his conduct and was "disqualified from serving upon Grand Juries in the future."[22]

John Slough's one-man crusade for judicial decorum provoked considerable complaint, particularly among attorneys, but neither they nor the partisan press suggested that he was guilty of misconduct at the time.[23] Certainly, his actions were unusual in New Mexico — stern, often intemperate, and occasionally unwise — but his efforts to reform the jury system were clearly justified. Even so, his authoritarian approach taught fear of the courts, not respect. Slough's manner and personal demeanor, rather than his decisions, prompted one attorney to denounce him as "the most overbearing, tyrannical, and unjust judge I ever saw."[24] That assessment was widely shared. Equally important, Slough's autocratic manner convinced the local authorities, who were used to doing things their way, that Slough was a threat to their power; among the ordinary folk who sat on juries, he gave the impression of being an Anglo tyrant.

In fact, the reforming zeal of New Mexico's chief justice was subordinated to the political scene that summer and fall of 1867. Events in Washington convinced many New Mexico Democrats and a variety of other interests that the time was right to take power away from the Republicans. With Andrew Johnson in the White House and a former Democrat as governor, the opposition to Chaves hoped to use local interests and support of Johnson's plan of Reconstruction to win back some of the critical votes they had lost. They chose as their candidate for Congress the enterprising attorney general of the territory, Charles P. Clever.

Charles Clever was a native of Prussia who emigrated to the United States in 1849. He settled in New Mexico the following year and began a determined effort to make his mark on the territory. He took employment as a bookkeeper with the firm of Eugene Lietensdorfer. The job gave him not only steady employment but also some important connections, including Joab Houghton. In 1854, Clever entered into a business partnership with Sigmund Seligmann. The partnership lasted for seven years, but by the time it was dissolved, Clever had already embraced new interests. In 1852, he briefly served as acting sheriff of Santa Fe County, and in 1858 he was appointed as U.S. Marshal for New Mexico. He also began reading law and in 1861 was admitted to the bar. His interests included part-ownership of the Santa Fe *New Mexican,* which he retained until November, 1863. In 1861, he was appointed adjutant general, and the following year he won the post of attorney general. He held both posts until 1865. When Connelly was removed, Clever lost the adjutant post, but he continued to serve as attorney general.[25]

Clever cast his lot with the Carleton faction in local politics and emerged from the Civil War as one of the leading opponents to the new Republican majority. Clever forcefully opposed Secretary Arny's assumption of power in 1866. By 1867, Clever was the logical man to oppose Chaves. He had strong credentials in New Mexico as one of the early settlers, prominence in the business community, and a reputation as an able attorney. The campaign for the delegate's seat was hard fought. Chaves confidently expected to win, but on September 2, 1867, Clever upset the incumbent.[26]

Chaves immediately challenged the election, claiming

widespread frauds and irregularities by the Democrats. He especially challenged activities of United States Marshal John Pratt and his deputies, who had responsibility for watching the polls. Prominent Republicans like William Breeden and R. M. Stephens charged that Pratt's deputies had intimidated Chaves's supporters and driven them from the polls. But the federal deputy at Albuquerque swore that a judge there had thrown out Clever votes, and Don Jesus Maria Baca y Salazar, brigadier general of the territorial militia, swore that many non-citizens had voted for Chaves.[27]

The importance of the territorial secretary, whose responsibility was to issue a certificate of election to the winner of the congressional seat, now became evident. Chaves's efforts to secure the post for Herman H. Heath suddenly became a matter of significance. Chaves fully expected Heath to give him the certificate.[28] But Clever's apparent majority caused the pliable secretary to hesitate. It was a critical blunder.

Governor Mitchell, by now an open supporter of Clever, moved into the breach and took the unprecedented step of certifying Clever's election. Heath compounded his error and implicitly endorsed Mitchell's irregular action when he signed the certificate and affixed the territorial seal. Chaves was mortified.[29] Realizing his mistake, Heath submitted a letter of protest with the certificate, but the damage was done. His timid conduct enraged Chaves, who demanded that Heath repudiate what he had done and prove that Chaves had actually won the election.

On October 1, 1867, Heath penned a lengthy letter to Schuyler Colfax, the Speaker of the House of Representatives at Washington, declaring Chaves to be the actual winner of the election. He claimed Clever's certificate to be invalid and his own role in the affair to be the result of political pressure from Governor Mitchell.[30] He followed this with a voluminous account of alleged frauds addressed to Henry L. Dawes, chairman of the House Committee on Territories. "I am the

political as well as the personal friend of Col. Chaves," he
admitted, but he insisted that his analysis of the election
reflected only his "sense of justice to an outraged people."[31]

New Mexico Republicans faced a critical moment. They
had returned majorities in both houses of the legislature
through the same election machinery that they alleged had
fraudulently elected Clever, so they were safe in their own
bailiwick, but now they were in danger of losing territorial
patronage. The election, which was to have been a demon-
stration of Republican strength, was an embarrassment.
Chaves had gone so far as to predict a "4,000 Majority with
safety."[32] Instead, he had to explain a stunning disappoint-
ment. He concluded that "the wealthy, the clergy, and the
toadies of the military" were the architects of a swindle.[33]

The Republicans had to move quickly and decisively to
prove the fraud, so Chaves departed for Washington to win
support for his challenge to the election. He arrived to find
the Radicals moving rapidly toward the impeachment and
expected removal of President Johnson. He conferred with
his political friends and altered his plan for an aggressive
fight. He advised Heath:

> You know that my intentions were, immediately upon my
> arrival here, to go to the different States, and make a
> personal call upon those friends who are most likely to be
> able to use a strong and powerful influence in my favor, but
> this plan has been overruled by our friends here who seem
> to think that such a course would show an anxiety which
> would be detrimental to our Cause.[34]

Chaves now planned to work quietly behind the scenes in
Washington, while Heath launched an aggressive campaign
at home. If Heath could demonstrate strength in New Mexico, Chaves believed he could cultivate favor with Washington's Radicals while hanging on to his presidential connection

Jose Francisco Chaves at Washington, D.C., during his days as claimant to the seat of territorial delegate. *Courtesy of the Library of Congress.*

as long as possible. He urged Heath to hold the line in the territory and handed him a monumental responsibility. He expected Heath to prove Democratic fraud in the election on a broad scale, to associate the Mitchell administration with the alleged fraud, to counter the attacks of the Santa Fe *Gazette,* and, most importantly, to pull the Republican legislature into a disciplined arm of the party.[35]

Heath, overwhelmed by the assignment and apparently still smarting from his earlier mistake, lacked Chaves's confidence. He nervously reported a rumor that Governor Mitchell intended to bribe the legislature into voting for statehood as a means of destroying the Republican hold on the territory. Chaves was unimpressed. He belittled the whole idea and assured his suddenly timid associate that Mitchell's crowd did not have "money Enough to give Away in a Canvass of that kind, and should it by chance result in carrying, the members of the first state Legislature will be of such a character that they will not be able to purchase them."[36]

Once reassured, Heath did not hesitate. He launched a vigorous effort in behalf of Chaves's claim to the delegate's seat, challenged the results of several contests for the legislature, and began to organize for the upcoming legislative session. The *New Mexican* assisted in the effort with a series of articles on "The *Gazette* as a loyal paper" that denounced the opposition as a bed of Copperheads.[37] As the *New Mexican* unleashed a veritable avalanche of charges against the Democrats, Heath and Chaves looked increasingly toward individuals who stood in the way of their plans. In his letter to Dawes, Heath stated flatly that "the Governor, Robert B. Mitchell, the Chief Justice, John P. Slough, and the Public Depositor [James L. Collins], were all active partisans of the Democratic candidate."[38]

The roles of Mitchell and Collins in the recent election were well known, but the *New Mexican* had never even hinted that Slough was a Democratic partisan. Even in his letter to Dawes, Heath failed to make a single specific charge against Slough, although he detailed several against both Mitchell and Collins.[39] Slough probably did support Clever. As attorney general, Clever had worked closely with Slough, and Chaves represented the very interests that Slough was challenging in his crusade for judicial reform. But Heath implied more. To prove his case, he had to provide evidence, and in the weeks that followed, public comments about Judge Slough shifted dramatically in both the *New Mexican* and in utterances by leading Republicans.

John Slough was an opinionated man, and he rarely kept his views to himself. That was enough to win him disfavor among the Republicans, but it did not prove him guilty of wrongdoing. In fact, proving him a partisan of the Democratic candidate would be enough if the Radicals had their way in Congress. Republican strategy was simple: Chaves and Heath saw in the rising mood in Washington an opportunity to consolidate their patronage position in New Mexico. The resignation of Justice Hubbell shortly before the election gave them a chance to improve their position in the territory's courts and encouraged Chaves's belief that the removal of just one more judge would give the Republicans a firm hold on the judiciary.

John Slough was vulnerable. His manner in the courtroom had antagonized many people. His forthright opinions were well known, and his profane displays of temper alienated many who might otherwise have supported him. Conveniently, in October of that year, Stephen B. Elkins registered his complaint about Slough's decision on the Comancheros. As a result, Slough soon found himself the subject of strong criticism.

Still, the attack against Slough came not because of his partisanship or his judicial behavior, but as a part of a design to unseat those federal officials who threatened the policies of Chaves and Heath. Slough had one quality they could not abide: independence of mind. He was stirring things up in the countryside and threatening the long-standing *modus vivendi,* with local factions critical to the Republican coalition.

As events unfolded, the design of Chaves and Heath became increasingly clear. They intended to capitalize on the prevailing mood in Washington. If they showed strong support for Radical policies and associated federal appointees with Democratic fraud, the New Mexico Republicans could secure not only the contested delegate's seat but the territorial patronage as well. Slough's partisanship in the election really did not matter. His general sympathies did. So, he, along with Mitchell, had to go.

Chaves apparently believed that a solid Republican judiciary would prevent further difficulties in election cases. He openly courted Perry E. Brocchus, the new federal appointee who would replace Justice Hubbell. Brocchus was not a newcomer to New Mexico or to the territory's bench. He was a suave, sophisticated man with great determination and a reputation as a fighter. In his younger days, he had denounced the Mormon church in a temple at Salt Lake City, with Brigham Young seated in the congregation.[40]

Chaves proudly informed Heath that Brocchus "is fully determined . . . to let everybody know that he is a firm, uncompromising friend of Chaves and of Chaves's friends." Moreover, early in November, Chaves instructed Heath to "have a law passed reorganizing the judicial districts, so as to give B[rocchus] Soccorro, Valencia, Bernalillo, Santana [sic] & Rio Arriba — he is agreable [sic], and that will give our friends R[io] A[rriba] in the next two years." He warned that the bill would have to be carefully managed. "This . . . is a matter of great importance," he wrote. "Brocchus is a firm and faithful friend of ours and will not allow the wanton prosecution of our friends which has been accustomed from time *immemorial* in this county by our foes."[41] Without judicial interference there, the great fund of Hispano votes in Rio Arriba would be secure. The grand design was taking shape.

CHAPTER 3

An Official Excitement

J ohn Slough remained blissfully unaware of the developing strategy of Jose Francisco Chaves and his associates. The resignation of Justice Hubbell had increased the responsibilities of the other judges, and Slough was busy making himself unpopular in Hubbell's district that October. The session in Bernalillo County passed uneventfully until October 14, 1867, when Slough summoned the Grand Jury before him and censured its members "for their failure to find true bills of Indictment in cases where the evidence warranted the same." Slough then dismissed the entire jury without pay. The next day Slough recanted and paid nine men who swore that they had not been guilty of misconduct. Then he abruptly terminated the October session of court.[1]

In explaining his actions, Slough declared:

> Perjury and false swearing being so frequent during the present term of this court, and by reason of the same, it appearing next to impossible to obtain a Jury of men of integrety [sic] and intelligence in the County in the brief period between this and the time fixed by law for termination of the Court, I feel it my duty to suddenly terminate my labours as Judge presiding in this district.

Slough declared that he had attempted to administer justice fairly and impartially. "My efforts in this direction have been resisted to such an extent by the causes referred to that to continue this Court here at this time is folly," he said. Then,

Slough added, "The peculiar legislation of the Territory which to so large an extent shields those who are disposed to rascality adds to my embarrasment [sic]."[2]

Slough's charges were probably well founded, but his selective dismissal of grand jurors opened him to further criticism that he was unfair and partisan, and his summary assessment of the intelligence and integrity of the citizenry hardly endeared him to the people there. Although court officers later swore that Slough instructed them to choose jurors without regard to party affiliation, Slough's actions convinced Republicans — who were looking for any excuse to attack him — that Slough was not the unswerving defender of justice that he pretended to be. His actions became the subject of street gossip in Santa Fe, and many attorneys reacted nervously to his use — or abuse — of his authority.[3]

Slough appeared to be unconscious of the growing mood against him. His plan to erect a memorial to New Mexico's Union dead captured most of his attention, and he participated in the cornerstone-laying ceremonies in Santa Fe.[4] Later, he and Governor Mitchell visited a new mining area. When they returned to the capital in late November, all seemed harmonious, and the Democratic *Gazette* thanked them for their interest in the territory's future.[5]

Then something happened that was remarkably fortunate for the Republicans. Guadalupe Mares, the man convicted of selling liquor to the Indians in defiance of efforts by Slough and the army to end such sales, appealed his case to Governor Mitchell, who pardoned Mares.[6] When Slough learned of the governor's decision, on the morning of November 27, he publicly exorcised Mitchell in terms that the *New Mexican* described as "more forcible than polite."[7]

Near noon, Slough found Mitchell in front of Steinberger's Drug Store on the plaza. Slough asked the governor for a minute of his time, but Mitchell coolly brushed Slough aside with the comment that it was his dinner hour. When the governor stopped a few steps away and talked at length with a group of men, Slough flew into a rage. He stormed into the office of the *New Mexican* and informed the startled proprietor that he would resign as chief justice.[8]

The more Slough talked, the more excited he became. Finally, he declared that he would go into the plaza and denounce Mitchell for all to hear. His friends tried to reason with him, but he could not be quieted. At the door of the newspaper office, Slough stopped, wheeled about, and swore that he had come to New Mexico in the first place because Mitchell had asked him to serve as chief justice. Now, he said, Mitchell could "take the Chief Justiceship and . . . stick it up his Royal Bengal a**."[9]

Back on the street, Slough continued his tirade against Mitchell. True to his threat, he dashed off his resignation letter and hand-delivered it to the local postmaster, after which he took out an advertisement in the *Gazette* announcing his intention to open a law practice in Santa Fe. He then resumed his mission of informing anyone who had not heard already that he "was no peon of Bob Mitchell."[10] "Indeed," gloated the *New Mexican,* "we are told by those who heard the Chief Justice that he excelled even himself in the line adopted by him."[11]

The next day Slough quietly recovered his letter of resignation from the postmaster and cancelled his advertisement with the *Gazette,* but his explosion still had Santa Fe buzzing when the legislature met. The "official excitement" was not over. Slough's outbursts had offended a great many people, and Heath and his friends moved quickly to take advantage of the windfall.

On December 2, 1867, when the legislature convened, "someone apparently bent on mischief" induced the solid Republican majority to ask H. H. Heath to administer the oath to the legislature — a prerogative traditionally reserved for the Chief Justice. The importance of the gesture was not lost on anyone in Santa Fe. With it, the Republican legislature expressed its disapproval of Slough and its support of Heath.[12] Slough assumed, correctly, that Heath, Arny, and Benedict had engineered the arrangement to insult him, and, already reeling from Mitchell's rebuff, he reacted exactly as his enemies expected.

That afternoon, Slough accosted Arny on the street and accused Arny of plotting against him. He denounced the former secretary as a liar, "a dirty dog," and "a damned dirty son of a bitch," to which Arny coolly replied, "I presume to be a gentleman which you are not: so far as calling me a damned liar is concerned you have done so once before and apologized within 3 days afterwards."[13]

With that Slough wheeled around and stalked away. As he walked across the street, Arny remarked to those standing nearby, "He is no gentleman, or he would not make use of such language on the public streets." The statement stopped Slough cold. Infuriated and shaking with anger, he turned on Arny again, screaming, "I will whip you in two minutes you God-damned son of a bitch." He seized the older man by the shoulder and raised his left hand as if to strike him, but Arny, with great presence of mind, shoved both hands into his pockets and said evenly, "I defy you to strike me, Judge; I dare you to strike me, Judge, I have no weapons, you dare not do it."[14]

Slough released Arny then and stormed away to continue his ravings in a nearby saloon. Arny's taunts had only heightened his anger, but the former secretary had played Slough perfectly. His coolness in the face of Slough's tirades won the respect of enemies as well as friends, while Slough embarrassed his warmest adherents. For most of the afternoon, Slough railed against Arny, Benedict, and Heath. He saved his choicest epithets for Heath, "that pusillanimous secretary of ours."[15] Slough was so irrational that he asked several men for a pistol so that he might be prepared for "those damned

William F.M. Arny, Republican leader whose confrontation with Slough helped precipitate the events that led to the judge's death. *Courtesy of Kansas State Historical Society, Topeka.*

sons of bitches." Late that evening he persuaded an army officer named J. Howe Watts to loan him a derringer.[16]

Slough's performance amazed his friends and pleased his enemies. His stern methods as a judge might have irritated many New Mexicans, but, in and of themselves, they did not provide a basis for removing him from office. His irrational behavior did. Ironically, his actions confirmed the absence of political guile in him, but they left him more vulnerable than ever. He had been a maverick who had not aligned himself with either faction. If he had been an open partisan, the Clever-Mitchell group might have come to his aid, but now he was a liability that the opposition was reluctant to adopt.

Heath had manipulated the affair beautifully. Having seen Slough's display in the Mares matter, he engineered the legislature's decision to have him swear in the body instead of Slough as a direct provocation. Slough had obliged his enemies beyond their expectations when he accosted Arny. He unwittingly provided the Republicans with the opportunity to secure his removal, and they quickly pressed their advantage. In a blistering editorial denouncing Slough's "disgusting and unmanly" attack on Arny, the *New Mexican* unveiled its new line:

> Hitherto, we have foreborne to speak of the many flagrant violations of propriety, manliness, and we may add decency, on the part of the Chief Justice of this Territory; but when he so far descends in the scale of manhood, as to exhibit himself upon the public streets of our city, blaspheming, assaulting, and by his coarse, vulgar, and consummately low language outrage the ears of the public, we can assure him and his friends that our forbearance further, would be justly construed into a neglect of the first duty of Journalists. Our lips are unsealed for the future.[17]

Arny, "desiring to avail himself of the benefits of the law," swore out a warrant against Slough.[18] The Republican leaders even dared hope that Slough could be stripped of his office with only token opposition from the Clever crowd. The possibilities were not far-fetched.

As Heath and Chaves had planned, the Republicans moved without delay to consolidate their power in the legislature and to prove Democratic fraud in the fall elections. Accordingly, when William Logan Rynerson, the Republican candidate for senator from Dona Ana County, presented himself at Santa Fe to challenge the election of Samuel J. Jones, the Democratic candidate to that post, the Legislative Council immediately took the challenge under advisement. The outcome was a foregone conclusion. Jones held a certificate of election from John Lemon, the probate judge of Dona Ana County, as the law prescribed; but after Heath had begun his "investigation" of the election returns, he had awarded similar certificates to Rynerson and two other representatives from Dona Ana County.[19]

The step was unprecedented, perhaps illegal, but Heath had assured Rynerson that there was "no earthly doubt" that he would be seated. Now Rynerson was in Santa Fe to claim his seat, and on December 5, 1867, over protests by Jones and the Democrats, who argued that Heath had no authority to issue certificates of election in the counties, a commission of council members informed Rynerson that he was a legal member of the council.[20]

An extremely tall man with a long, flowing beard, William Logan Rynerson was a Kentuckian by birth. He had attended Franklin College in Indiana and received another kind of education in the California mining camps. His career in New Mexico dated back to 1862, when he arrived in the territory with Carleton's "California Column."[21] His attachment to Carleton did not prevent him from being accused of misconduct (although it may have contributed to the charges being dropped), nor from pursuing an independent course in business and politics.[22] As a staff officer, he invested heavily in southern New Mexico mining properties and cultivated important friendships. When he was mustered out at Mesilla in November 1866, he already enjoyed significant influence in Dona Ana County.

In a county that was traditionally strongly Democratic, Rynerson threw his political support to the Republicans. He attracted the attention of Republican leaders in June 1867 in a dramatic confrontation with Clever supporters at Las Cruces. At the local nominating convention, Rynerson attempted to nominate Chaves for the delegate's seat, but the presiding officer, a Clever man, refused to recognize him, whereupon Rynerson led Chaves supporters out of the hall and into the street and there nominated Chaves. Reportedly, more than three hundred Chaves supporters rallied outside while a mere handful of Cleverites remained in the meeting. Rynerson was then named to a committee to nominate Chaves supporters for local offices. This committee, consisting of nine Hispanos and four Anglos, nominated Rynerson for senator.[23] Now, in Santa Fe, he took his seat in the Legislative Council as the only Anglo member and as a man with a considerable political debt to pay. He did not know Judge Slough, but from that moment their futures were linked.

Despite Heath's successes so far, his position was not yet secure. On the day after Heath swore in the legislature, that body took the precaution of having the probate judge of Santa Fe County readminister the oath — which implicitly confirmed Democratic charges of misconduct. Rumor had it that the legislative leaders had discussed the matter with Mitchell who, "being a Sloughite," refused "to recognize them as organized on the grounds that they had not been properly qualified." Reportedly, the Attorney General agreed, so they had the task done again by the local probate judge.[24] Clearly, the unity of the Republican party in the legislature was tenuous. A council with a clear Republican majority debated the issue of Rynerson's seat for two days before accepting Heath's certificate.[25]

The Democrats were already railing against the "monstrous usurpations of Heath" when news reached Santa Fe of Heath's letter to Schuyler Colfax declaring Chaves to be the legally elected delegate. They now made an issue of Heath's statement that he had been forced to sign Clever's certificate, and some cracks appeared in Republican solidarity. Leading Republicans complained bitterly that Heath did not give Chaves "a clear certificate without any explanation."[26] Of course, Heath could not have done that under the law, but the secretary suddenly found himself on the defensive, and, in the words of one observer, "the Sloughites and Cleverites now made their's a joint cause."[27]

On the night of December 3, the Democrats held a rally and chose a committee to question Heath on the matter of Clever's certificate. The next day, Heath agreed to answer their questions in writing. That night, the Democrats reconvened to hear Judge Slough tell what he knew about the subject. "I was present when the votes were counted and shortly after the Hon. C. P. Clever was declared elected as Delegate to the Congress of the United States," he said, adding:

> I went to the office of H[is] E[xcellency], the Governor, and heard the said Heath asking H. E., the Governor, for a written statement that the Hon. C. P. Clever had been elected to said office by a majority and that he, Heath, was satisfied that he had really received said majority. I then asked Mr. Heath whether he wanted that letter of statement from the Governor for the purpose of giving another certificate to Chaves or some other person to which he responded in a categoric manner "that he would give no other certificate."[28]

On the following day, a committee of three men presented the questions to Heath, who informed them that he would answer "when he thought it convenient to do so" and ushered them out of his office.[29]

In another part of the city that same morning, Judge Slough was arraigned on a charge of "assault and battery" in the confrontation with Arny. His case was then called immediately and was to be heard before Abram Ortiz, a local justice of the peace. "The hall was crowded to overflowing," a Colorado correspondent reported. "Neither Riston, the tragedian, or Dickens, the lecturer, could have drawn such a crowded house as did Arny and Slough."[30] After Arny had testified, a string of witnesses including Governor Mitchell and Attorney General Merrill Ashurst swore that Arny's reputation was bad and that he was a known liar.

Even as Ashurst testified, "this farce was suddenly brought to a close, by a sudden and unexpected tableau." In the midst of the proceedings, Slough abruptly stood up and demanded of Justice Ortiz if it were not true that Ortiz "was bound over some few weeks since, to answer a charge of perjury and malfeasance." When the Justice admitted that it was true, Slough ripped apart his papers, grabbed his hat, and swore that he would not be tried in Ortiz's court. He then stormed out of the courtroom.[31]

"The court was astonished," the *New Mexican* reported:

> The officers of the court stood dumb with amazement. The assembled populace were alarmed to see so little respect paid to a court — even a humble one — by the highest judge in the Territory, and every man who witnessed Judge Slough's conduct on this occasion properly denounced it as an outrage upon law, and the dignity of the courts of law.

The *New Mexican's* only regret was that Ortiz did not have

Slough arrested "until he learned what belonged to the dignity of a court."[32]

Slough was now convinced that he was the object of a conspiracy. He wrote "A Card to the Public" in which he attempted to explain his side of the controversy. He said that Heath and Arny, "both claiming at the time to be friendly to me," engineered the insult in the legislature. He denounced both men, then apologized for the excitement caused by his conduct and pleaded "an excitable and natural indignation at a great unnecessary insult as my excuse."[33]

But he could not let the matter go. In words less polite than his prepared remarks to the Democrats and the public, Slough declared:

> If Gen. Heath said he allowed himself to be forced to sign Clever's certificate, he was a coward — for no man but a coward would allow himself to be forced. And that when Gen. Heath asserted that Mr. Chaves received 1,206 votes majority over Mr. Clever he was a damned liar; and that when he attempts to heap insults and indignities upon me, as in the swearing in of the legislature, he was a damned son of a bitch; I have denounced him here now as I have on the public streets, and I have been expecting to receive a challenge from him, but I understand the damned coward is going to the papers, and if he does, I will treat him with contempt, as he deserves to be.[34]

On the night of December 5, the Democrats issued a statement condemning Heath, but the next day the legislature passed a glowing tribute to him.[35] While Heath was reveling in this victory, Slough was back in Ortiz's court, where he agreed to appear in District Court during the next session to face charges.[36] As the *New Mexican* hurled new barbs at Slough and as Heath protested the "undignified and flagrant conduct of the chief justice" to Washington, the Republican legislature reminded the community of Slough's public spectacle with a law prohibiting the use of profane and blasphemous language on the streets of Santa Fe.[37] But the final insult was yet to come. Heath complained about Slough to the assistant attorney general of the United States, writing that "it is probable that the legislature will pass upon the matter."[38]

Of course, Heath had already begun the process of securing Slough's removal. He had authored a series of resolutions condemning the chief justice's behavior. Shortly after Slough's altercation with Arny, Heath approached Don Jesus Maria Pacheco, one of the most respected members of the Legislative Council, and asked him to introduce the resolutions. Pacheco reviewed them, then asked Heath to translate them into Spanish so that he could read the resolutions more carefully. After studying them, Pacheco decided that he did not want the responsibility, and he passed his copies of Heath's resolutions to William Logan Rynerson.[39] Rynerson did not hesitate. He owed Heath his seat.

At that time, however, he did not know Slough personally, so he spent several days investigating the judge. Rynerson found plenty of evidence of Slough's ill temper and frequent use of profanity, but little else.[40] On December 7, Rynerson was assigned to the judiciary committee of the council.[41] When the next issue of the *New Mexican* appeared on December 10, the editors warned:

> This man Slough has carried altogether too high a hand since he has been in this Territory, and now he has been "picked up" on it. We advise him to moderate his conduct, and descend from his high stilts, and [we] believe this certain fact, that he is no more than other men, and much less than most of them.[42]

The next morning, Rynerson introduced his resolutions, which contended that Slough "in no respect rises to the dignity of his position as such Chief Justice, and possesses none of the attributes which should attach to a man in his exalted position." Eleven specific charges followed:

1st. As a magistrate, he is tyrannical, overbearing, and frequently unjust.

2nd. He has, at times, imprisoned jurors who . . . have failed to render verdicts in accordance with his own expressed views and wishes.

3rd. He has imposed fines upon jurors amounting to their entire pay . . . because they refused to follow his instructions. . . .

4th. He has . . . conducted himself in so arbitrary a manner in his courts, as to intimidate the juries in their boxes, and so flagrant, at times, have been these exhibitions of his tyranny, that members of the bar . . . have in court openly informed him that the juries held him in fear, and would condemn or acquit prisoners as desired by him. . . .

5th. He brings with him upon the bench, not unfrequently, political antipathies and partizan sentiments, and in some cases has acted in chambers as the politician rather than the Judge.

6th. He brings discredit upon his profession and his judicial character, by frequently exhibiting himself before the people so under the direct influence of ardent spirits, as to appear more the bully than the Judge. . . .

7th. He has entered public offices and assaulted, in vulgar and blasphemous terms, officers and employees of the military service, and he has committed an assault and battery upon at least one such person without provocation.

8th. [. . .] he has, in the coarsest and most violent terms, denounced the Governor and other high officials of the Territory, upon the public streets of Santa Fe.

9th. [. . .] he attacked a Federal officer, venerable in years, in a most outrageous and unmanly way, and being

These have already passed the Council. They will pass the House on Monday or Tuesday next

H.H.H.

No. 2.

Joint Resolution of the Legislature of New Mexico.

WHEREAS, In the opinion of this Legislature, the judiciary among a people, provided as it is for the securing of justice and the protection of the rights of the people, should, so far as the Judges belonging thereto are concerned, possess the confidence of the people; that the Judges themselves should be men of good example to the community, preserve the dignity of their station, promote the morals of the people, and so act before the world as to assure it that Justice and Morality, Law and Order, Truth and Dignity, are the prerequisites of that man who stands between man and his God; and

WHEREAS, The Chief Justice of this Territory, JOHN P. SLOUGH, fails in every essential particular to represent the above character, and in no respect rises to the dignity of his position as such Chief Justice, and possesses none of the attributes which should attach to a man in his exalted position; and

WHEREAS, It is the duty of this Legislature to make known to the Federal authorities, under which New Mexico exists as a Territory, the disabilities under which our people rest with respect to the Chief Justiceship of this Territory, we enumerate the following, as among the grave charges which it is our duty, as legislators, to make against John P. Slough, Chief Justice of New Mexico:

1st. As a magistrate, he is tyrannical, overbearing, and frequently unjust.

2d. He has, at times, imprisoned jurors who, under their oaths as such, have failed to render verdicts in accordance with his own expressed views and wishes.

3d. He has imposed fines upon jurors amounting to their entire pay as jurors at the terms at which they were serving, because they refused to follow his instructions in finding verdicts.

4th. He has, at various times, conducted himself in so arbitrary a manner in his courts, as to intimidate the juries in their boxes, and so flagrant, at times, have been these exhibitions of his tyranny, that members of the bar, in duty to their clients, have in court openly informed him that the juries held him in fear, and would condemn or acquit prisoners as desired by him, the said Chief Justice, from the bench.

5th. He brings with him upon the bench, not unfrequently, political antipathies and partizan sentiments, and in some cases has acted at chambers as the politician rather than the Judge.

6th. He brings discredit upon his profession and his judicial character, by frequently exhibiting himself before the people so under the direct influence of ardent spirits, as to appear more the bully than the Judge, and members of the two houses of the Legislature have themselves witnessed these exhibitions.

7th. He has entered public offices and assaulted, in vulgar and blasphemous terms, officers and employees of the military service, and he has committed an assault and battery upon at least one such person, without provocation.

8th. Within the immediate knowledge of the members of this Legislature, he has, in the coarsest and most violent terms, denounced the Governor and other high officials of the Territory, upon the public streets of Santa Fe.

9th. Within the hearing and the knowledge, personal, of many of the members of this Legislature, he attacked a Federal officer, venerable in years, in a most outrageous and unmanly way, and, being much excited, he made himself on this especial occasion, the object of much disgust on all sides.

10th. When arrested and brought before a magistrate for examination for the aforesaid criminal assault, he refused to be so examined, and whilst in arrest, before such magistrate, he violated his arrest by abruptly leaving the court in the midst of the examination.

11th. That said John P. Slough is now under bonds to answer at the proper tribunal for the said offense, much to the discredit of the dignity of the bench of this Territory, and to the mortification of the people of New Mexico. Wherefore,

Be it Resolved by the Senate and House of Representatives of the Territory of New Mexico. That, in the opinion of the people of New Mexico, John P. Slough, Chief Justice, should be removed from his place as such Chief Justice, for the foregoing and for other reasons not herein enumerated, and his place filled by another Judge who regards the sanctity of the judicial office; who respects the sentiments of the people; who deserves, by good conduct, the respect of the people, and who shall merit, by his high character as a jurist, the confidence of the people.

Resolved, That a copy of this resolution be transmitted respectively to His Excellency the President of the United States, the Attorney General of the United States, the presiding officer of each House of the Congress of the United States, and to the chairman of each Committee on Judiciary in the two houses of Congress, and to the Hon. J. Francisco Chaves, at Washington.

The Joint Resolutions of the New Mexico legislature calling for the removal of Judge Slough. This document precipitated the Slough-Rynerson quarrel that resulted in Slough's death. Note the comment signed "H.H.H." written by Herman Heath. *Courtesy of the National Archives, Washington, D.C.*

much excited, he made himself on the especial occasion the object of much disgust on all sides.

10th. When arrested and brought before a magistrate for examination for the aforesaid criminal assault, he refused to be so examined, and whilst in arrest, before such magistrate, he violated his arrest by abruptly leaving the court in the midst of the examination.

11th. That said John P. Slough is now under bonds to answer at the proper tribunal for the said offense, much to the discredit of the dignity of the bench of this Territory, and to the mortification of the people of New Mexico.[43]

The Rynerson resolutions concluded with an appeal for Slough's removal from office. News of the effort soon made its way to the streets of Santa Fe and to Judge Slough. At first he was so shaken that he could scarcely discuss the subject, but as he talked to friends and colleagues, his temper flared. If some of the charges had some basis in fact, Slough was highly incensed at charges of drunkenness and partisanship on the bench. He sought out several attorneys and court officials and demanded to know if they knew anything that would support the charges. They assured him that they did not. Slough then demanded that "his friends in the Chaves party" block the resolutions. If they failed to do so, he warned, "I am a politician from this act."[44] Stephen B. Elkins, Merrill Ashurst, and Slough's clerk, Peter Connelly, wrote letters attesting to Slough's fairness as a judge. And in the Legislative Council, Felipe Sanchez valiantly tried to delay action on the resolutions. He failed.[45] On Saturday, December 14, the resolutions passed the council by a vote of ten to two, and Heath confidently predicted that the assembly would follow suit on Monday or Tuesday of the next week.[46] So far, the plan was working smoothly.

Late that afternoon Slough made his way to the Exchange Hotel (the La Fonda), where Rynerson and most other public

Preamble and Resolutions

Of the two Houses of the Legislature of New Mexico, Passed, unanimously, December 6 and 7, 1867.

WHEREAS, It has come to the knowledge of this body that public meetings have been held at Santa Fe, within a few days past, denunciatory of General H. H. Heath, the Secretary of this Territory, which denunciations result solely from antagonism to the manner in which the said General Heath has performed his duties as such Secretary; and

WHEREAS, The official conduct of the said General Heath has been, in the opinion of this Body, both correct and proper, and in accordance with right and justice, and especially so far as his action in the results of the late election in this Territory is concerned; therefore

Resolved, That, in the opinion of this Body, General H. H. Heath is eminently worthy of the confidence of this Body, and of the entire people of New Mexico; that in him we recognize an honest and faithful public officer, faithful to the people and the laws, and that all his official acts, since he became Secretary of this Territory, meet with the cordial approval and approbation of this Body.

Resolved, That the Speaker of this House do transmit one copy each of the above preamble and resolutions, signed by the officers of this House, authenticated under the seal of this Territory, to His Excellency the President of the United States; to the Secretary of State of the United States; to the President of the United States Senate, the Speaker of the House of Representatives of the United States, and to the Hon. Richard Yates, Chairman of the Committee on Territories in the Senate of the United States, to the Hon. James M. Ashley, Chairman of the Committee on Territories in the House of Representatives of the United States, and to the Hon. J. Francisco Chaves.

ANASTACIO SANDOVAL,
President of the Council.
FRANCISCO P. ABREU,
Speaker House of Reps.

RAFAEL CHACON,
Secretary of the Council.
FRANCISCO SALAZAR,
Chief Clerk House of Representatives.

A true Copy:
H. H. Heath,
Secy. New Mexico

Resolutions supporting Herman H. Heath and his conduct as secretary of New Mexico passed by the New Mexico legislature, December 1867. *Courtesy of the National Archives, Washington, D.C.*

officials boarded during the legislative sessions. The judge
entered the billiard room and sat down on a sofa near Rynerson, who was shooting pool. Turning to the person next to
him, a surveyor named Hill, Slough belittled Rynerson as a
"son of a bitch and a thief." When he got no response, he
moved to another seat and said in a loud voice, "There is a
strange combination, but one which you frequently see in this
world, a gentleman associated with a damned thief. I illude
[*sic*] to that 7-foot son-of-a-bitch playing with Col. Kenzie —
he is a damned lying thief and a coward but the damned
scoundrel has not the courage to take it up." Slough also
suggested that Rynerson wear a collar inscribed "I am
Heath's dog."[47]

When no confrontation followed, Slough left the room. As
he passed out the door, he met Don Celso Baca, the senator
from San Miguel County. Baca greeted Slough, but the judge
snapped back, "don't speak to me you son of a bitch." Slough
then cornered MacDonald, the proprietor of the hotel, and
said to him, "That damned Rynerson; I have been trying to
pick a quarrel with him, but he wouldn't pay no attention to
me, and I had that man Hill rubbing up against him, but he
couldn't succeed."[48]

After Slough left, MacDonald pulled Rynerson aside and
asked if he was armed. Rynerson said that he was not and
asked why MacDonald wanted to know. MacDonald then
related his conversation with Slough. Rynerson thanked him
and returned to the billiard room, where several other men
related what Slough had said about Rynerson.[49] The judge
had by then left the building, and Rynerson went looking for
him. In front of Green's saloon, Rynerson met Merrill Ashurst. Unaware of what was happening, Ashurst asked if
Rynerson was going to the Masonic meeting that evening.
Rynerson said, "I don't know whether I shall or not. I am
looking for Judge Slough — have you seen him?" Ashurst said
that he had seen Slough a few minutes earlier in front of the

Seligmann & Brothers store. Rynerson hurried to the store, but did not find the judge. He eventually gave up the search and went to the lodge meeting.[50]

Chief Justice Slough was deeply shaken by the resolutions. On Sunday morning he did not attend church with his family as was his usual habit. Instead, he left home early, talked with Peter Connelly, and wrote a few letters in his office.[51] Sometime after eleven o'clock, he left his office and walked to the Exchange Hotel. He had several drinks — one witness later said "more than usual," although MacDonald said the judge "seemed to be merely passing the time; did not observe him drinking much." He was strangely quiet. Later, Samuel Duncan came in, and he and Slough spent more than an hour in earnest conversation.[52]

A few blocks away, James L. Collins, the federal depositor, sat at his desk, scribbling a letter to the attorney general of the United States concerning the "set of slanderous resolutions" against Slough. "This movement against Judge Slough," he wrote, "is the work of H. H. Heath and Kirby Benedict, late Chief Justice of the Territory who was removed by Mr. Johnson to give place to Judge Slough." As he warmed to the subject, Collins grew increasingly indignant:

> The official character of Judge Slough, and the manner in which he has discharged his duties as Chief Justice of the Territory, will be fully endorsed by several members of the Bar, who have practiced in his Courts. I will say however that he is the only Chief Justice we have had since the organization of the Territory who had firmness and force of character sufficient to require the observance and execution of the laws. This has been attended with much difficulty, especially as regards the Juries. Persons serving in juries had been indulged so long in disregarding the law, and the instructions of the Court, that Judge Slough in his determination to correct this, has been subjected to much

criticism and abuse, of which the above parties have availed themselves to facilitate the passage of the Resolutions.[53]

As Collins wrote, a sudden pounding on the door interrupted his thoughts. He opened the door to an excited friend who brought a terrible message: *Judge Slough had been shot.*

William Rynerson had a room at the house of Mrs. Sena, near the Exchange Hotel. At about 12:45 in the afternoon, Colonel Francisco Abreu, the Speaker of the territory's House of Representatives, who also roomed at the Sena house, came out of his room and met Rynerson at the front door. "Let's go to dinner," Abreu said. "It is hardly time yet," Rynerson replied, "and I have a little business to attend to."[54]

Rynerson arrived at the Exchange Hotel shortly before one o'clock that afternoon, dressed in black and wearing a heavy overcoat draped over his shoulders like a cape. He politely refused an invitation to take a drink and stood quietly beside the fireplace in the bar. When the dinner gong sounded, the boarders filed through the billiard room and into the dining room, but Rynerson remained at his post by the fireplace, as though waiting for someone. A few minutes later, Slough came out of Samuel Duncan's room, still engaged in serious conversation with Duncan. In the billiard room, Duncan paused to speak to the hotel owner, and Slough walked on into the bar. Suddenly, there was loud talking and then a shot.

Rynerson stopped Slough at the door as he entered the bar and demanded a retraction of his insults.

"What did I say?" Slough inquired.

"You called me a son of a bitch and a thief," Rynerson replied.

"I won't take it back," Slough said.

"If you don't take it back, I will shoot you."

At that instant, Rynerson raised a Colt's revolver from

beneath his coat and repeated his demand. Slough, who was standing with both hands in his vest pockets, carefully withdrew his left, extended it, and said quietly as he stepped toward Rynerson, "take care, take care. Don't shoot."

"Take it back, or I'll shoot you," Rynerson said evenly.

"Shoot and be damned!" Slough stormed back.

The shot came instantly. Slough turned as if to avoid it. As the bullet penetrated his left side a few inches above his hip, Slough's right hand jerked from his vest, and a derringer, loaded, capped, but not cocked, slipped from his fingers to the floor. As Rynerson tried to cock his revolver again, Santiago L. Hubbell, one of Slough's friends, grabbed Rynerson, and the two men crashed into the billiard room. Hubbell demanded that Rynerson hand over his gun. Rynerson at first refused to surrender the revolver, but when Van C. Smith, a prominent lawyer, stepped in and asked him for the pistol, Rynerson gave it to him.[55]

By this time the boarders were crowding around Slough. Daniel Tappan asked Slough where he was hit, and Slough said, "In the side — send for a doctor." Seeing little blood, Tappan tried to reassure the judge, telling him he appeared to have been hit in the hip and was not badly hurt. Slough knew better. "Yes I am," he said. "Send for a doctor." McDonald, who had picked up Slough's derringer, and others carried Slough into an adjoining room, where several doctors examined him while he puffed on a cigar. The bullet had torn into his side and ranged through his intestines. The doctors agreed that he was mortally wounded.[56]

Rynerson surrendered himself to Sheriff Jose D. Sena, but later that afternoon John Pratt, the United States Marshal, took custody of the prisoner and with a military escort transferred him to the guardhouse at Fort Marcy. Death came for John Potts Slough shortly before seven o'clock on the morning of December 17, 1867. As the news spread

Santa Fe. East San Francisco Street with view looking east. The Exchange Hotel, or La Fonda, is at the right. Sketch by Theodore R. Davis, ca. 1866, from *Harper's Weekly Magazine. Courtesy of Museum of New Mexico. Neg. no. 31339.*

through the town, a considerable crowd gathered, and enough lynch talk circulated around the plaza that Sena swore in a number of local merchants as deputy sheriffs.[57] These precautions prevented a riot, but during Rynerson's transfer from civilian to military custody, Slough's grief-stricken, ten-year-old son slipped up behind Rynerson armed with a pistol and would have shot him had one of the guards not seen him in time to prevent it.[58]

The chief justice of New Mexico's Supreme Court had been shot down by a member of the Legislative Council. And yet, John Slough's passing was strangely incidental in the politically charged expressions of regret and compassion that flooded from the pens of public officials and the presses of the Santa Fe newspapers. John Slough's death precipitated an even more bitter partisan struggle, and those who hoped that sober reflection would result from the tragedy hoped in vain.

CHAPTER 4

The Trial of John P. Slough

By the time James L. Collins returned to his unfinished letter, John Slough's fate was certain. Collins took up his pen again and scribbled a lengthy postscript. He told the Attorney General that he had written originally to vindicate Slough from the "foul slanders" that were "fabricated" by enemies of the judge. "They hoped that the endorsement of these false charges by the Legislative Assembly would effect the removal of Judge Slough," Collins wrote, "and then, by a further action of these pliable bodies, to secure the reappointment of Benedict to the position." Before finishing the letter, he added, he had been told that the judge had been assassinated. "In this manner they created the vacancy which they so much desired, and now it is understood that they intend to urge the name of Benedict to fill the vacancy." Collins then made a bold accusation:

> The death of Judge Slough has cast a gloom over the people that has never before been witnessed in this community, and has prepared us to look with suspicion upon everything that can be construed into the semblance of a combination against his life; and while we would not willingly do injustice to Judge Benedict, it is not improper to state that he was roomed with the assassin until a late hour of the night before the murder was committed.[1]

The Collins letter concluded with an appeal that Slough's replacement be "some good lawyer, who is not a resident of

New Mexico." "If made from the friends of either party," he added, "it will only tend to keep open the feud which now unfortunately exists." Governor Mitchell endorsed the letter and suggested the name of Robert Burns of Kansas as a replacement.[2]

The Collins epistle was merely the first in a litany of protests. The Democrats wasted no time in seizing the killing of Judge Slough as a cudgel against the Republicans. "The shooting of Judge Slough is pronounced by all who saw it as a most foul cold blooded assassination, and the result of a conspiracy to get rid of him on the bench," Governor Mitchell wrote. "Judge Slough was the only Chief Justice that ever has enforced the law in this Territory without fear[,] favor or affection — and the result is his death."[3] In Washington, Clever, the delegate apparent, praised Slough as "an honest, fearless, and upright judge who introduced many wise and salutary reforms in the administration of Justice in the Territory."[4] "All things taken in connection," the *Gazette* concluded, "lead to the conviction that there was a conspiracy against the Judge."[5]

As the arguments unfolded, however, Collins's accusations against Benedict proved to be unfounded. If Benedict had been considered as a possible replacement for Slough, Slough's assassination killed his chances. As Collins put it, "Under these circumstances if he allows his name to be used in connection with the appointment, it will certainly leave room for unfriendly comments."[6] In fact, no evidence ever emerged to support the accusations against Benedict, and they faded without further comment.

Upon reflection, the Democrats and the friends of Slough saw Heath's hand in the alleged conspiracy, and it was the secretary who found himself damned "as the prime mover of the difficulty which resulted in the death of Judge Slough."[7] When Clever was seated in Congress as the apparent winner in the delegate contest, he wrote the attorney general:

It is my firm conviction that these troubles and the present disorganized and dangerous state of feeling in the Territory are attributable solely to the reckless and lawless proceedings of the Secretary, and that unless he is speedily removed from his official position, it is impossible to foretell the consequences that may ensue.[8]

On January 2, 1868, Clever was even more direct in a letter to Secretary of State William H. Seward that amounted to a bill of indictment against Heath not only for his role in the death of Slough but also for his conduct in the delegate election, his swearing in of the legislature, and his action in giving Rynerson a certificate of election after the probate court in Dona Ana County had given the certificate to Rynerson's opponent, Samuel Jones.[9]

In meetings throughout the territory, Heath was condemned for his conduct as secretary. On New Year's Eve, he was burned in effigy in Las Vegas with a placard about the neck that read:

I am H. H. Heath
Don't hurt me
I was forced to sign that certificate[10]

An eyewitness described the scene: "The torch was applied and as the flame blazed and cracked around him, the General looked down upon his persecutors with stoic indifference nor uttered a word of reproach nor cry of anguish."[11]

At a meeting in Santa Fe on December 19, Heath was condemned as the author of the removal resolutions against Slough. Heath had "by his perverse and mischievous machinations already indirectly caused the death of Slough, . . . and the course he is now pursuing tends to lead to the assassination or murder of other citizens."[12] The clamor against Heath was so great that his life was threatened. "For four days &

Herman H. Heath, the volatile secretary of New Mexico and bitter enemy of John Slough. *Courtesy of the Library of Congress.*

nights my house had to be guarded," he wrote. "I could not appear upon the streets unattended; I was threatened with secret assassination by the suppporters of Gov. Mitchell, and a guard of police attends my house nightly."[13]

Against the background of moral outrage over Slough's death, the Democrats increasingly pressured the now-vulnerable Republicans. Governor Mitchell used his veto power with abandon, and when the legislature tried to limit his powers, he vetoed that effort, too, refusing to approve their memorial asking for restrictions on his power because of the "agitated, personal and unsound legislation" of the legislature.[14] Clever used his position in Congress to promote the appointment of John S. Watts as Slough's successor.[15] The *Gazette* kept up a barrage of accusations against Heath and ridiculed Chaves's switch to Radical principles.[16] And always, the specter of conspiracy and assassination loomed in editorial and correspondence.

The Republicans were not idle in all of this. On December 17, 1867, the day that Slough died, Heath wrote J. M. Binckley, the assistant attorney general, announcing Slough's death as the result of a "personal difficulty" between Slough and Rynerson. His version of the shooting followed:

The Resolutions were introduced, I think, on Thursday of last week, and passed by a large majority on Saturday. On the evening of the latter day, Judge S made a most violent attack upon the reputation of Capt. Rynerson; it being of the most serious character, part of which Capt. R heard. On the following morning, Capt. R met the Judge, informed him that he was fully advised of the bitter attack made upon him, and of what he had said, and requested him to retract. This the Judge declined to do and stepped toward Capt. R menacingly, drawing a Derringer pistol from his pocket. Before he had time to shoot, Capt. Rynerson drew his revolver and shot the Judge. The wound was made in the front part of the abdomen, as I learn, and terminated in the melancholy manner noted above.

I have been a little particular in giving you the history of this case, because, from motives well understood here, other parties may color the case differently. Judge S. had been acting very intemperately both in words and conduct for two weeks; being chagrined because the Legislature requested me to administer the oath of office to its members instead of himself. He had spoken very severely of myself, but I forbore to notice it, and when he was finally shot, the community was not surprised, however much it was regretted.[17]

For the moment, however, Heath stood largely alone. Chaves, Benedict, Arny, and the other visible leaders kept their silence. Elkins did remind the attorney general that a vacancy existed because of Slough's demise, but his motivation seemed to be to avoid a disruption of the courts.[18] Even the *New Mexican* initially moved cautiously. Responding to the *Gazette's* initial attack in December, the editors declared:

> The time to address ourselves to the task which the *Gazette* has unnecessarily and in bad taste imposed upon us, will be after the examination of Capt. Rynerson, before the civil tribunals, when the passions and prejudices of the public mind have subsided, and men shall be better able to think calmly upon the occurrence in question; — we shall respect too, the feelings of a bereaved family, to whom our sympathies are naturally due.[19]

A Denver correspondent did advise the Cincinnati *Commercial* on December 24, that while he did not "presume to pass judgment upon the action of the deceased," the evidence suggested that "the conduct of Rynerson was justified." "Slough was a very irritable man," he added, "and gave way to his temper upon little provocation."[20] Still, the simple reality was that Rynerson had greatly embarrassed, perhaps even scuttled, the Republicans' plan, and they concluded that discretion was the best course. That left Heath to take the brunt of the attack.

Early in January 1868, a letter appeared in several newspapers in the East written by an unnamed army officer (who later turned out to be J. Howe Watts) to M. A. Slough in Cincinnati on the day Judge Slough died. The officer reported that Slough had been shot "without any blame on his part" by a man who hardly knew him. He added:

> H. H. Heath . . . was the real cause and instigator of the act,
> for the Judge and Rynerson did not know each other three
> weeks ago. The Judge denounced Heath for an insult put on
> him as Chief Justice, and Heath, not having the manhood
> to come forward and fight his own battles, pressured Ryner-
> son to introduce into the Senate a set of resolutions against
> the Judge. The Judge then denounced Rynerson very justly
> and naturally, to his face. Rynerson did not resent it then,
> but came next day with a pistol and shot the judge.[21]

The editor of the Council Bluffs *Nonpareil,* which published the letter, added, "We have known H. H. Heath for
three years past, and from our personal knowledge of the
man, we have not the slightest doubt of the truth of the
foregoing statement."[22] The Dubuque *Herald* sounded a similar note about the secretary, described by the editor as "too
much of a coward to maintain his own quarrel":

> A private letter received in this city says that Heath is
> compelled to keep a guard about his house and person to
> protect him from summary vengeance, and it is added that
> he will certainly be killed if he remains in Santa Fe. There
> are few who know him hereabouts who will write for him to
> leave. His connection with the murder of Slough is only
> characteristic of the man, and perhaps no more appropriate
> instrument of vengeance can be found than the outlaws of
> New Mexico.[23]

The Atchison, Kansas, *Champion* provided additional remarks about "that disreputable and unconscionable shyster
General? H. H. Heath." The *Champion's* Republican Radical
editor added a more blistering indictment:

> Heath is the sublimated essence of all that is false, treach-

erous, mean and shystering. He is utterly incapable of an honest impulse or a decent action. The people of this State have a lively recollection of the shyster and his name is never mentioned without an expression of contempt and hatred.[24]

The violence of the verbal attacks surprised Heath. The beleaguered secretary wrote a friend:

Being prominent in my influence with the legislature, and having more influence with its members than suited the purposes of my opponents, an effort was made, totally at variance with reason or sense by them to connect *my* name with the transaction [Slough's death] & I was threatened with mobbing and assassination.[25]

While he was reeling from the threats and public protests, Heath received a telegram from Chaves, informing him that the House Committee on the Territories had voted against Chaves in the election dispute. Chaves, who had escaped the calumny heaped on Heath and who had been specifically absolved by the *Gazette* as "an honorable and true man," blamed the unfavorable vote on Heath's action in signing Clever's certificate.[26]

That was more than Heath could take. "Under the law I could not give you a clean certificate," he wrote angrily to Chaves. "It was impossible for me to do so, without stultifying myself before the law, which requires the Secretary to issue a certificate to the person receiving the highest number of votes." His anger boiled over. "I have run the gauntlet of abuse . . . for giving you what I did. . . . But for doing this, I have been pursued by the assassins of the other party, whom you well know as such . . . so that I am forced to go armed day and night; and at night my friends never allow me to go even from my office, unattended."[27]

Slough's death put the Republicans on the defensive, and in late December and early January the party leadership indulged in a round of finger-pointing, as each official tried to clear his own skirts and to shift blame for the situation to someone else. But Heath and Chaves were too shrewd to allow such unproductive activity to long deter them. Slough's demise was embarassing, if not unfortunate, but it could not be allowed to divert attention from more important issues. The shooting of the chief justice had to be played down. The official view was that the judge's intemperate behavior was the cause of his death and that Rynerson had killed him in self-defense.

Early in January, Chaves quietly suggested that Perry Brocchus be given Slough's position, but he did not push the nomination. With Brocchus even then en route to New Mexico to assume his seat as associate justice of the court, Chaves was confident and comfortable. He advised Heath not to hurry the nomination of a replacement for Slough, suggesting that delay would work in their favor if they could, in the interim, secure the congressional seat.[28] Unfortunately, Heath and other New Mexico Republicans had already recommended the appointment of R. H. Tompkins to the post. Chaves warily and half-heartedly promised to support the nomination, but he warned that he could not "be hopeful of a successful result" because of Clever's acceptance as "defact [*sic*] Delegate."[29]

Chaves took charge, reminding his colleagues that everything depended upon a satisfactory settlement of the election contest. "There is but one thing that we can do . . . to demoralize our political enemies beyond redemption for the next four years," he wrote Heath, "and that is to secure my seat."[30] He chided Benedict and Elkins for not gathering testimony on the election frauds and prodded them to get to the task quickly.[31] The strained relationship between Governor Mitchell and the legislature afforded another opportunity to push the Chaves cause. "Mitchell feels shaky in his boots," Heath assured Arny early in January, and within days a series of resolutions demanding the governor's removal were introduced.[32]

The resolutions attacked Mitchell for replacing Arny's appointees early in 1867 and for his frequent use of the veto, but three of the seven charges related directly to the election of 1867. Mitchell was accused of naming "a Delegate to the Fortieth (40th) Congress of the United States, while a canvass of voters for said Delegate was in progress in this Territory," of improperly establishing new election precincts (a right reserved to the legislature), and of issuing an election certificate to Clever in violation of the law.[33] The mood in the legislature hinted that the resolutions would pass, and Heath began to suggest discreetly that he would be a suitable replacement.[34] Three days later, on January 17, the legislature established a joint commission to investigate the election of 1867. On January 28, the legislature approved the report of the election committee. Predictably, the report concluded that Democratic frauds had denied Chaves his seat.[35]

These tactics restored Republican momentum. Arny was in Washington to help Chaves. The Republican majority in the legislature had the situation at home well in hand. Benedict, Elkins, and Heath were busily gathering testimony on the election frauds. And the Republicans had joined Chaves in supporting Judge Brocchus for chief justice and Colonel W. H. Russell for associate justice to replace Brocchus. A fresh optimism characterized the correspondence of the party leadership. Chaves, so recently considered a favorite of Andrew Johnson, saw Johnson's impeachment as the salvation of New Mexico Republicans, and he confidently predicted that the President would be removed.[36]

John Slough's death at the hands of William Rynerson was rapidly slipping into the background. In the flurry of political machinations, only one act of a bipartisan nature marked his passing. The Santa Fe Bar Association adopted a series of resolutions concerning Slough's death, drafted by a committee that included such prominent Republicans as Stephen B. Elkins, A. M. Tompkins, and T. L. Snyder. The resolutions stated in part: "it affords us pleasure to testify to his magnanimity of character and to his liberal and obliging disposition as a man, and as a fair and impartial arbiter upon the Bench."[37] This simple endorsement stood in sharp contrast to the emotionally charged pronouncements of the politicians, and it carried weight because both Republicans and Democrats participated in the gesture.

Rynerson's courtroom appearances seemed strangely trivial in all of this. A preliminary hearing convened before Judge Joab Houghton on Friday, January 3, 1868. Merrill Ashurst represented the Territory, while Judge Benedict and Stephen Elkins represented Rynerson. One by one, the witnesses detailed the events at the Exchange Hotel on the evening of December 14 and the fatal encounter of December 15.[38]

On the essential facts, the testimony was remarkably consistent. Slough did go to the hotel on the evening of December 14. He did make disparaging remarks about Rynerson in an apparent attempt to precipitate a confrontation. He did leave without succeeding. Several men did tell Rynerson what Slough had said, and Rynerson did go looking for Slough without finding him that evening. All of the testimony concerning the incidents in the billiard room came from witnesses for the defense, but the prosecution failed to shake their portrait of the irate judge looking for trouble.

The testimony confirmed that Slough did not attend church on the morning of the shooting as was his usual custom, but instead worked in his office for a time before going to the Exchange. In contrast to the previous evening, he seemed subdued and spent most of his time in discussion with Samuel Duncan — about what, Duncan never said.

While Slough was closeted with Duncan, Rynerson ar-

Joab Houghton, Slough's associate on the bench of New Mexico and the judge who presided over the preliminary hearing in the Slough murder case. *Courtesy of New Mexico State University Library, Rio Grande Historical Collections.*

rived at the hotel and took his station in the bar, pacing back and forth as if waiting for someone. When the gong sounded for dinner, he kept his post beside the fireplace in the bar until Slough entered the room. Rynerson demanded a retraction of the statements Slough had made the night before. Slough refused. Rynerson pulled a revolver and repeated his demand. Slough again refused, and Rynerson fired, mortally wounding Slough.

On all of that, the testimony agreed to a surprising degree. Only two significant points of difference arose. Daniel Tappan testified that he "saw Judge Slough in [the] bar room nearly all morning and he was drinking more than usual — he insisted that McDonald and myself should drink, which he had never done before, and I remarked he was getting liberal." In contrast, McDonald testified, "I only saw Slough in there [the hotel bar] once, about 9 or 10 o'clock — did not notice him drinking."

The witnesses agreed that Rynerson pulled his revolver on Slough while the judge was facing Rynerson, standing about four feet away with his hands in his vest pockets. However, they differed on what Judge Slough did at that point and on when Rynerson fired. Daniel Tappan swore:

> [I] saw Rynerson with a pistol in his hand as I was going to dinner and heard him say "will you take it back?" The Judge made no direct answer but advanced a few steps with right hand in pocket and left extended, and said, take care, don't shoot. Rynerson said again, take it back. The Judge turned a little and said I don't propose to take anything back, and at that moment Rynerson fired and the Judge fell on the floor. I heard something fall and saw it was a Derringer. . . . Did not see Judge Slough draw pistol, but heard it fall and McDonald picked it up before I got there.

R. M. Stephens swore:

Rynerson drew his pistol and said "if you don't take it back
I'll shoot you" — Judge Slough then turned round his left
side and either put his hand in his pocket or was going to
and said shoot and be d — d or shoot d — n you. . . . Did not
see any movement of Judge Slough when Rynerson fired as
to putting his hand in his pocket.

Santiago L. Hubbell, who had tried to take the gun away
from Rynerson after the shooting, swore:

Rynerson had the muzzle of the pistol in one hand trying to
cock it, and approached about a step, and Slough said hold,
hold don't shoot — at the moment of the firing, and when he
fell, Judge Slough drew his hand from his pocket, as with a
spasmodic effort, from which a Derringer fell. . . . When
Rynerson said take it back or I'll shoot you, the second time,
he had his pistol in his hand and presented — Slough had
his hand in his pocket. . . .

Jacob Gold swore: "I was within three quarters of a yard of
them — saw no Derringer. . . . saw nothing in Judge Slough's
hand — saw his hand in his pocket." Mr. Conway swore:

Judge Slough took both hands from his pockets, and with
his left hand extended and said, hold! hold! and then
Rynerson fired. Judge Slough stood a second or two before
he fell, his right hand holding a pistol. . . . I saw the pistol;
it was a very small one and covered by his hand. I think it
was a Derringer or small pocket pistol — saw it drop on the
floor. . . . When Slough drew his hand from his pocket [he]
had his pistol. I saw no motion as if to cock or use it — only
saw the muzzle of the pistol.

Under cross-examination, Conway added, "Slough's hands
were in his pockets at the time Rynerson's pistol was leveled

at him and then it was he jerked his hand out of his pocket."
T. McDonald swore:

> I heard a pistol fire — stepped into the barroom to see who
> had fired — found it was Rynerson — Hubbell was trying to
> get the pistol from him. I turned then and as I did so Slough
> dropped and a small Derringer fell from his hand which I
> picked up and put in my pocket. . . . The Derringer was
> loaded and capped but not cocked. . . .

Van C. Smith swore:

> [I] heard Slough say he would not or did not propose to
> retract, and at the same time put his hand in his pocket and
> took one or two steps toward Rynerson and someone
> stepped before me, or the casing of the door concealed him
> from me and then I heard the pistol fire and saw Slough
> fall. . . . Judge Slough had his hand in his pocket and
> seemed to clutch something and raised it about half way
> out . . . [but] did not see Rynerson have anything in his
> hand."

Following a series of character witnesses for Rynerson,
the attorneys began their summations on the afternoon of
Monday, January 6. The closing arguments continued
through the next day. That afternoon, Judge Houghton ruled
simply: "I will not say that the proof [of guilt] is evident, but
the presumption is great, and the prisoner is remanded to
jail, without bail."[39]

On January 14, 1868, the *New Mexican* published the
proceedings of Rynerson's hearing and broke its self-imposed
silence on the death of John Slough. With the preliminary
hearing completed and with Slough's family departed, the
editors declared that "our duty is now due to Capt. Rynerson,
and to the public alone, and we purpose to discharge that
duty faithfully, earnestly, and with fidelity." Then followed a

detailed vindication of Rynerson, "a deeply injured man," primarily by means of a blistering indictment of Slough.

After his denunciation of Mitchell, the editors said, Slough had fallen "into a wholesale system of abuse, invective, [and] traduction [*sic*], which finally resulted in the only way known in this country, in such cases, fatally at the hands of a man who dared resent it." The editorial continued with a blend of the factual and the fanciful:

> Few, if any, of Judge Slough's political opponents escaped his violent tongue. The grossest and most obscene scurrility was heaped, by his ever voluble tongue, upon many of the first citizens of the territory, and upon some of the federal officials as well as the legislature. Men were forced to go armed day and night, ready to defend themselves, lest they should be murderously attacked by him, for he was known to generally carry a pair of Derringer pistols in his pockets, contrary to territorial statutes, and for which breach of law, he had, upon the bench, fined many a man.[40]

If Slough had appeared irrational and irresponsible to many, the *New Mexican* now portrayed him as a malevolent monster. "Surrounding himself with bad men, and not guarding himself at all times from a too free indulgence in stimulants; goaded on by partizan [*sic*] harpies, who thought it a splendid affair to have a Chief Justice as a companion, and under their influence, the days passed on."[41]

When Rynerson introduced the resolutions for Slough's removal, he did so without malice, the editors avowed, and Slough had no "cause of quarrel" with him. Yet, he sought out Rynerson with the intention of provoking a fight. Slough had enlisted the aid of "a man named Hill," who, the *New Mexican* insisted, had been "inseparable from Slough for some days prior to this" and who had been promised Peter Connelly's post as clerk of court for his services. What evidence existed to support this charge, the paper neglected to explain.

Instead, the editors insisted that Slough had for weeks said about town that "there should be a funeral and he would furnish the corpse."[42] The paper's account of the shooting itself portrayed Rynerson as a man who, by chance, encountered the judge, demanded a retraction, and was forced to shoot him because he "was unwilling to see his reputation attacked and destroyed by the means employed by Judge Slough."[43] Slough's death, the editors asserted, was the consequence of Slough's unseemly attack on Rynerson's honor. The *New Mexican* editors then made the political opposition into the "instigators" and agitators of the quarrel. J. Howe Watts was blamed for loaning his derringer to Slough, conveniently overlooking the fact that Slough had obtained the pistol days before the dispute with Rynerson and the way in which this bit of information contradicted the *New Mexican's* own assertion that Slough *always* went armed with a brace of derringers — presumably his own. Judge Houghton was accused of political partisanship because he did not rush back from Fort Union before Christmas to hear Rynerson's case, and for remanding Rynerson to jail when he was "perfectly justifed" in killing Slough.[44] The paper predicted that no jury would ever find him guilty of any crime in the matter.

This editorial provoked an angry response from John T. Russell of the *Gazette*. "The *New Mexican* in its extreme anxiety to justify the murder of the late lamented Chief Justice Slough and exculpate Rynerson, does injustice to the deceased, to the state of society in New Mexico, to Judge Houghton . . . and to Rynerson himself." Russell was particularly pointed in reference to Slough:

> Judge Slough was highly esteemed by the people of the Territory as an honest, upright and incorruptible officer. The small knot of Chavez [*sic*] politicians in and about Santa Fe were the only ones who disliked him, and they did

so because he abolished the corruptions which had grown up in the administration of Justice under the auspices of his predecessor, who was of their party. No person anticipated the violent death of the deceased, except perhaps these politicians.[45]

Russell went on to excoriate the *New Mexican* for condoning violence and for attacking Judge Houghton: "All who know Judge Houghton, and he has lived in the Territory for a quarter of a century, will do him the justice to say that in the discharge of his official duty he acts with entire impartiality and without fear, favor or affection."[46]

On January 12, Perry Brocchus reached Santa Fe to take up his duties as associate justice. "Judge Brocchus arrived yesterday, and is attending the Supreme Court term," Heath advised J. M. Binckley, the assistant attorney general. "He was warmly received and we are glad of his arrival. He was needed, and came in good time."[47] That was an understatement.

On January 16, Captain Rynerson applied for a writ of *habeas corpus* before the new associate. Brocchus convened a hearing at ten o'clock the next morning.[48] Sheriff Sena advised Judge Brocchus that Rynerson was being held on the strength of a commitment for the crime of murder that was signed by Peter Connelly, the court clerk. Rynerson's lawyers then argued that the commitment did not identify specifically the murder or any facts about the murder their client was alleged to have committed and that it was not signed by any magistrate with legal jurisdiction.

The attorney general moved that the commitment be amended to show that Judge Houghton had committed Rynerson to jail for the murder of Judge Slough. Brocchus overruled the motion. Ashurst then proposed that Rynerson be discharged because of the problems with the commitment and then be rearrested on the charge of murdering Judge

Slough. Brocchus denied that motion, too. Either of the procedures recommended by Ashurst would have settled the questions identified in the application and won at least temporary
release for Rynerson. But, inexplicably, Brocchus chose not to
follow either course. Instead, all of the parties, including the
prosecution, agreed to proceed by "going into the merits of the
case without any change in the form of proceeding."[49]
Brocchus never explained why the merits of the case were at
issue in a *habeas corpus* hearing, especially in light of the
technicalities that would have freed Rynerson, but obviously
he was determined to take testimony and to make a decision
on something more than points of law.

Then, in another unusual move, all parties agreed to
accept the testimony taken before Judge Houghton as correct
"without the calling of witnesses who testified, except by way
of explanation of testimony taken." Even in territorial New
Mexico, this action was legally questionable.[50] Once these
maneuvers were completed, the prosecution began what
turned out to be a bizarre and ill-advised course.

Ashurst called only one witness — Rafael Chacon, the
chief clerk of the Legislative Council.[51] When Chacon had
been sworn in, Ashurst introduced in evidence Rynerson's
resolutions. The defense objected on the grounds that the
resolutions were irrelevant. Ashurst argued that the resolutions were relevant because they provoked the confrontation
between Rynerson and Slough. Elkins and Benedict said that
they would consent only if they were allowed to present
testimony concerning the truth of the charges against
Slough. Brocchus allowed the resolutions to be introduced,
but he ruled that facts proving the truthfulness of the resolutions would also be admitted.

Once this wrangling was over, Ashurst asked Chacon a
single question: "Is this book now before you the journal of
the proceedings of the Legislative Council?" Chacon replied
that it was, and Ashurst turned the witness over to cross-ex-

Merrill Ashurst, the attorney general of New Mexico who prosecuted William Rynerson in Judge Slough's death. *Courtesy of the Museum of New Mexico. Neg. no. 6989.*

amination. When Rynerson's lawyers had asked a few simple questions about the details of the debate over the resolutions and Rynerson's demeanor in presenting them, Ashurst asked Chacon if Rynerson had brought copies of the court records to the council to support his charges. Chacon said no, and the Attorney General closed his case, noting that he had one more witness who had not arrived and asking permission to examine the witness if he did show up.

Rynerson's lawyers could hardly believe Ashurst's course of action. Almost miraculously, Slough's conduct, not Rynerson's, had become the issue. Virtually all of the testimony that followed concerned Slough's character, as though the truth of the resolutions was the test of Rynerson's guilt or innocence. This peculiar tactic failed to directly confront the issue of Rynerson's act of violence, but it proved to be a stroke of good luck for Rynerson. A case against Slough now could be built in court under oath and used to vindicate his killer.

The first witness called by Elkins and Benedict was Joseph Purcell, an employee of the Chief Commissary in Santa Fe, who testified that Rynerson had met with him about a confrontation between Purcell and Slough. Purcell explained that Slough had come to his office at the commissary some days earlier and demanded to know what he had said to Slough's daughter. Purcell said that he had told Slough that he had asked the little girl to "go home and quit abusing my dogs." Slough, Purcell said, had retorted, "You God damned little son of a bitch, if you talk to my daughter in that way I will thresh the s*** out of you."

At that point, Purcell recalled, a Mr. Barta, another employee of the commissary, asked Slough who he was talking to, to which Slough replied, "To him, God damned him, if he chose to take it up." Barta then told Slough to get out. According to Purcell, Slough refused to leave, swore that the commissary was a public office, and struck Barta. Two army officers then seized Slough and escorted him to the door.

Slough attempted to apologize, but the apology was refused, and Slough blew up again, swearing, "You God damned little son of a bitch, I will shoot your brains out on this placita; I will shoot you on sight."[52]

H. C. "Clay" Carson, the bailiff of the Supreme Court and acting deputy sheriff for Santa Fe County, recounted Slough's "violent, coarse, and blasphemous" denunciation of Heath and other public officials after Heath swore in the legislature. He testified that he believed Slough to have been under the influence of liquor when he confronted Heath, "for if he had been duly sober, I don't think he would have used such language. . . . I have seen Judge Slough so under the influence of intoxicating drinks as to forget himself and his sense of propriety." Thomas S. Tucker, an editor of the *New Mexican,* then testified concerning Slough's threat to resign the chief justiceship after the Mares pardon.[53]

And so the testimony continued. H. H. Heath testified but briefly, swearing that he had never "had any personal difficulty or unfriendly words with Judge Slough," although he had heard rumors that Slough had used abusive language about him on the streets. L. D. Fuller recounted the confrontation between Slough and Arny, supported by testimony from Don Jesus Maria Pacheco, Eben Everett, and Antonio Ortiz y Salazar. Slough's minister, Reverend McFarland, then took the stand and testified that Slough had missed church on the morning of the shooting, which was rare, and that his absence was even more striking because the service was a special one in which the ordinance of the Lord's Supper was observed.

Next, Peter Connelly, clerk of the U.S. District Court, took the stand. Under close questioning, Connelly reviewed Slough's decisions and a variety of courtroom actions that Rynerson had examined before introducing the resolutions. He had told Rynerson that because of his relationship with Slough, Connelly would have refused to show Rynerson the records if he could have done so. Connelly then testified that after the resolutions had passed, Slough came to his office very angry: "Judge Slough told me that he looked to his friends in the Chavez [*sic*] party to stop the passage of the resolutions and intimated that he would hold them responsible if they did not, mentioning my name and Mr. Elkins. This interview created some anxiety in my mind."

Rynerson's lawyers followed with a series of witnesses who testified to Slough's tyrannical behavior as a judge. Severo Baca, justice of the peace, probate judge, and senator from San Miguel County; Henry Henrie, an Albuquerque lawyer; and Jose Sena, sheriff of Santa Fe County and deputy U.S. Marshal, led off the litany. Afterward, Stephen B. Elkins stepped out of his role as lawyer and took the stand as a witness.

Elkins recounted some of Slough's actions on the bench that had aroused concern and caused comment, then came to the question of Slough's political partisanship. He recalled a conversation he'd had with the judge in Mora County on election day the previous autumn. Slough had asked him, Elkins said, if a man could vote out of the county in which he resided. The two men examined the law together, and Elkins told Slough he believed that it was lawful. Slough disagreed, and an argument ensued in which Elkins told Slough that he would vote outside his county of residence and defy anyone to "draw an indictment that would stick." Slough then swore that if Elkins did vote, he would be indicted and fined $500 if convicted. Elkins retorted that he would take that risk and vote anyway, to which Slough replied, "Well if you vote, I will strike you from the list of the members of the Bar; I will disbar you." Elkins then said, "Judge, this a very serious question now, and your proposition to disbar me affects materially the interests of other men confided to me, as also my own interests and I would have to reflect over the question as to whether I would vote or not."

Under cross-examination Elkins said that he had voted
that day and that Slough had not. He also swore that he
"would not be willing to state that I know of any official act of
Judge Slough's that was governed by his political opinion."
Under re-examination, he recalled a conversation with
Slough that transpired after the Rynerson resolutions had
been introduced. Slough had bluntly inquired if Elkins knew
anything that would support charges of drunkenness and
partisanship. Elkins told him he did not. Slough then em-
phatically told Elkins that he expected Elkins and his other
friends in the Chaves party to stop the resolutions.

Elkins quoted Slough as saying, "If the resolutions pass, I
am a politician from this date; my first act will be to surround
myself with those who support me politically; I will at once
discharge Peter Connelly, the Clerk, although I have nothing
against him; I know him to be a good clerk; but he and you
should not allow me to be unjustly abused." Elkins told him
that he could not affect the legislature's vote and begged him
not to hold Connelly responsible. Elkins said that Slough left
the office in a "friendly manner" but still insisted that he
would carry out his intentions.

Elkins testified that he had then written a letter to the
U.S. attorney general, declaring that he knew of nothing that
would support charges of drunkenness or partisanship on the
bench on the part of Judge Slough but asking that he be
excused from commenting on other points.[54]

After Francisco Abreu testified briefly about his conversation with Rynerson on the day of the shooting, the defense
called Merrill Ashurst, the prosecutor, to the stand. Even he
testified that he had told Rynerson that he "would not oppose
the passage of the resolutions nor do anything to hinder the
removal of Judge Slough." Ashurst then swore that he was
still "much aggrieved" over one of Slough's decisions. He also
testified that Slough had told him that if the resolutions
passed, Slough would become the partisan judge he was ac-

cused of being. He added, "I will also state that Judge Slough in moments of excitement often said things that in his cooler momonto ho did not attompt to oarry out."

Ashurst even admitted that he had remarked in times past that Slough "was the most overbearing Judge I had ever met" and that this view was common among lawyers who appeared in Slough's court. The defense next asked Ashurst what he knew of Rynerson's character, to which the prosecuting attorney replied, "I think I know Capt. Rynerson's general character as a man of peace and good order — it is good. . . . The opinion formed of Capt. Rynerson is that he is a remarkably quiet man." Under cross-examination, Ashurst swore that he had "never seen anything of a partisan nature about [Slough]," that in Slough's actions "his purpose was always for the correction of existing evils," and that he had never seen Slough drunk on the bench. But when Ashurst stepped down, he had done considerable damage to the Territory's case.

R. H. Tompkins, an attorney already being promoted as Slough's successor by Heath, followed Ashurst with a particularly harsh assessment of Slough's performance: "My opinion is that the arbitrary and tyrannical manner of Judge Slough operated in many instances to defeat the administration of pure justice." Tompkins continued, "I think I have seen signs of political animosity and partisan feeling in his conduct upon the Bench; so much so as to control his action; but still I cannot state such was the fact, but I was induced to the belief and am still of the same belief." Tompkins's testimony was damning:

> I cannot say that I ever saw Judge Slough drunk, but upon several occasions, I have seen him so under the influence of intoxicating drink that he had said things for which he was afterwards sorry. I was of the opinion that his impulsive nature was such as to cause him, when under the least

influence of spirits, to lose entire self control, when anything was said or done which he thought touched his integrity or honor.

R. M. Stephens testified briefly about the shooting of
Judge Slough — the only witness to do so. Henry Herring
appeared as a character witness for Rynerson, and the hearing was over.

It had been an incredible performance. Pursuing the trail
that Ashurst had laid out for them, Rynerson's attorneys had
drawn a frightening portrait of Slough as a disturbed and
irrational man. In contrast, the witnesses for the defense had
testified again and again to Rynerson's good character and
had insisted that his presentation of the resolutions to the
legislature was done without any personal animosity toward
Slough. Completely lost in the process was any consideration
of Rynerson's culpability in the death of the judge.

Now it was time for Brocchus to act, and he disappointed
no one. He presented a long and detailed interpretation of the
events surrounding Judge Slough's death. After first explaining how the legislative resolutions came to be the focus of the
hearing, he launched into a flowery discourse on why it had
been necessary to consider the truthfulness of the resolutions
against Slough despite impulses "to spread the mantle of
oblivion over the faults and errors of the dead." The judge
decreed that Ashurst's intent had been "to show malice on the
part of the petitioner towards the deceased, and thus to open
a fountain of malevolence to be followed on, in its vengeful
flow, until in that fatal conflict, it took its angry confluence in
human blood."

Brocchus then said flatly that the testimony confirmed
the truth of the allegations against Slough contained in the
resolutions, which were passed, he said, "by an almost unanimous vote" by men who were "prompted by a confident belief
in the truthfulness of the charges." Brocchus declared that

the testimony demonstrated that "it cannot reasonably be maintained that the introduction and advocacy of said proceedings by the petitioner, in his legislative capacity, offered evidence of malice on his part toward the deceased."

Following this, Brocchus began a reconstruction of events based on the testimony taken in the preliminary hearing before Judge Houghton. He made much of the lack of conflict in the testimony and noted particularly that no attempt had been made "to impeach the credibility, or disparage the veracity of a single witness," conveniently overlooking the preliminary character of the hearing before Judge Houghton.[55] Rynerson had, in fact, killed Slough, Brocchus declared, and "acts of such a sad nature are never willfully committed without some strong motive; some powerful incentive." His duty, he said, was to discover the motive that led Rynerson to his act of violence. Why that was his duty in a *habeas corpus* hearing he did not explain.

The judge's frame of reference soon became clear, as he droned on:

> While the law . . . holds him who, with malice aforethought, takes away the life of a fellow man, guilty even to the forfeiture of his own life, yet, tempered by mercy, it looks with compassion on human infirmity and regards with indulgence the weakness of the human heart, when wrought upon by the impulses of sudden and violent passion which have their rise in a deep and vehement sense of personal wrong.

"In that spirit," as Judge Brocchus put it, he recounted the events that led to the shooting. Of Slough's failure to attend church Brocchus make much: It was Slough's custom to attend Sunday services and unusual that he would miss the special observance of the Lord's Supper scheduled for that day. Apparently, a set of legislative resolutions that attacked his integrity, called him a drunkard and a tyrant, and threatened to end his career was insufficient reason for interrupting Slough's usual habits. Brocchus also emphasized the testimony of the single witness who had avowed that Slough had been drinking more than usual on the day of the shooting. He portrayed Slough as a man bent on a fight from the previous evening right up until the fatal confrontation with Rynerson. His view of Rynerson was more forgiving; he depicted the defendant as "a man of delicate sensibilities, high intellectual culture, and unimpeachable honor and respectability."

Finally, Brocchus came to the argument he would use to set Rynerson free. If, he said, Rynerson had heard Slough's insults and had shot Slough "at the moment of their utterance" then no impartial jury in the land would have convicted Rynerson of murder in the first degree. The law, he said, "looks with compassion on the infirmity of human passion when it suddenly results from a sense of wrong or a deep and poignant sense of wounded honor." He admitted, however, that in this case time had elapsed between the insult and the shooting, and time usually restrains passions. "But," Brocchus continued,

> there are some wounds that never heal; some passions that never die. If there are such wounds and such passions, where shall we look for them, but in the breast of the man of honor when assailed by calumnies that tend to rob him of his reputation and good name, which are no less dear than life? But assuming that the grievance was such that a few hours of reflection might, in the contemplation of reason, have softened or subdued them, the question arises, whether or not the manner of the deceased, when called on by the petitioner for a retraction, did not amount to an aggravated repetition of the insult, and did not open anew

and afresh the wound at first inflicted. If it did, then the accused was put in precisely the attitude towards the deceased in which he would have stood, had he heard the utterance of the offensive language, and resented it with death, on the spot. The law would not have held him guiltless then, but its stern justice would have been softened by its merciful regard of human frailty, and he would have been held, in the eye of the law, as well as the sight of his fellow man, guiltless of that degree of crime against society which demands the expiation of death.

Rynerson had "hurried a fellow mortal before the great bar of eternal justice," and he would have to answer for that before a jury, the judge explained. Brocchus concluded with an impassioned appeal to the rule of law and for the importance of the courts in protecting the rights of citizens and in assuring the progress of the West. He then ordered Rynerson released on $20,000 bond.[56] The Brocchus decision was an incredible piece of work. Writing in the lofty style for which he was well known, the judge had virtually exonerated Rynerson while managing to maintain an illusion of fairness. The least that could be said was that he had gone far beyond his duty in a *habeas corpus* matter.

Merrill Ashurst, the attorney general of New Mexico, recognized the potential impact of the publication of the Brocchus decision on the future course of the case and urged the judge not to publish it "so that the public mind may not be prejudiced by any decision that he made."[57] However, Brocchus's opinion was published in the *New Mexican* on January 28, 1868, accompanied by an editorial that practically canonized the judge. "In his integrity and justice," the editors intoned, "the people hope."[58] The public's response to the decision confirmed Ashurst's fears; within days, the *Weekly Arizonian* reported that the *habeas corpus* hearing "exculpates Rynerson from blame." "There is but one construction to be put upon the matter," the newspaper concluded. "Judge Slough sought to kill Capt. Rynerson and got killed himself."[59]

The political implications of the Brocchus opinion were obvious. Governor Mitchell and James Collins promptly mailed a copy of the decision to the attorney general in Washington. "In view of the infamous and imponderable course of Judge Brocchus in this case," they wrote, "we would most respectfully request that a Chief Justice be sent out with as little delay as possible, and that in no event should Brocchus be allowed to preside over the final trial of this murderer."[60] Ashurst added his protest to the "unpardonable and unjustifiable" actions of the new justice.[61]

Even so, the Brocchus decision elated New Mexico Republicans. Arny sent a glowing tribute to Washington, and Stephen Elkins reported to Chaves that "the important case of Rynerson on Habeas Corpus came before him [Brocchus], which he patiently heard and rendered a decision that reflects honer [*sic*] upon him as an able judge, and pleases everyone."[62]

"We seem to be sailing before the wind," Heath exulted as January closed. "Rynerson is bailed by Brocchus; the Legislature has reported vs. Bobbie M. and adopted a report on the election frauds; and the legislature has solemnly asked for Bobbie's removal. *Entre nous* — look out for the governorship."[63] The impeachment of Andrew Johnson seemed certain, and with the Radical Republicans controlling Congress, Chaves's seat would be granted and vacancies in the territorial offices would be filled with loyal Republicans. Confident now, the Republicans accelerated their support of Brocchus for the chief justiceship. With the courts in hand, the Republicans would at last be secure.

CHAPTER 5

Justice — of a Sort

John Slough's widow departed Santa Fe with her children in January 1868, quietly returning to the bosom of her family in Ohio.[1] She carried her bitterness with her. On February 18, from her brother's home in Cincinnati, she appealed to Salmon P. Chase, the chief justice of the United States Supreme Court, to help her. "You are aware of the cruel, unjust manner in which my husband has been taken from me, and though I feel not the spirit of revenge my affliction seems almost more than I can bear," she wrote. "And I feel that justice must be done me, and my fatherless children, in avengement of the wrong that has been done us. In your high judicial power, I felt you might affect much in regard to the man (Rynerson) who committed the rash deed and whose unwarranted course cannot go unpunished." She continued:

> It seems at this time in New Mexico, that principle is sacrificed by party feeling, which seems to rule all action. And, I feel, that this sacrifice is too great, to be decided by men of prejudice. One of the Judges, Judge Houghton, will I am satisfied act conscientiously. The other, Judge Brochus [*sic*], has already been influenced by the man, H. H. Heath, whom I believe to be the instigator of my husbands [*sic*] death, and whose dishonest course has made him obnoxious to all honorable citizens. . . . Both (Rynerson & Heath) were comparative strangers to my husband, their social position being such as to exclude them from society, at least with

those who knew their dishonorable reputations. They first insulted [him] by introducing grossly false resolutions against my husband, which he with his manly impulses denounced openly to the aggressors, but with a knowledge of their own dishonor, they did not resent the accusations put upon them, but selected a time when my husband least expected, to perpetrate the horrid deed.[2]

Chase could do little more than sympathize, but he forwarded the letter to the attorney general, who already had on his desk a letter from Mrs. Slough's brother, A. C. McLean.[3] No one in Washington even attempted to intervene in the case. John Slough was a victim without a champion, and his family found no relief in their efforts to see Rynerson punished and Slough's reputation vindicated. The family's grief was extended when an insurance company refused to pay off Slough's $5,000 policy because of the circumstances of his death. Mrs. Slough took the case to court and eventually won a settlement.[4]

The Rynerson case moved inexorably toward a different result. During the February term of the district court, a Santa Fe County Grand Jury chaired by Robert M. Stephens (himself a witness in the case) returned an indictment against Rynerson for murder.[5] On March 3, 1868, Samuel Ellison, acting on behalf of Merrill Ashurst, who was incapacitated because of surgery, asked for a continuance to the next term of court. The judge postponed a decision until March 6, when he denied the motion.[6] Then Rynerson's attorneys asked for a change of venue to San Miguel County, arguing that Rynerson could not receive a fair trial in Santa Fe, Rio Arriba, and Santa Ana counties because "the jurors . . . have been . . . so prejudiced against him . . . by reason of party spirit."[7] The change of venue was granted, and Rynerson's case was transferred from Santa Fe to Las Vegas — and Judge Brocchus's court.

John Potts Slough during his days as military governor of Alexandria, Virginia, looking every inch the dignified and stern administrator. *Courtesy of the Henry E. Huntington Library and Gallery, San Marino, California.*

When the trial began on March 17, the outcome was no longer seriously in doubt. Merrill Ashurst fought with the only weapons he had left. He applied for a continuance because of his surgery. Brocchus denied the motion. Ashurst then requested a continuance because three key prosecution

witnesses, James Hubbell, James T. Johnson, and Samuel
Duncan, had failed to appear for the trial. Ashurst pleaded
that Johnson and Hubbell would testify that Rynerson had
attempted to shoot Slough again as he lay on the floor and
that Duncan would testify that he and Slough had been
discussing private business until a few moments before the
fatal encounter — which would establish that Slough was not
there looking for trouble. Despite Ashurst's plea that no other
witnesses could provide this critical testimony, Brocchus denied the motion.[8]

Ashurst then requested yet another change of venue "for
the reason that men of influence in said county, friends of
said defendant have been and still are so prejudicing the
minds of the people of said county and jurors in favor of said
defendant . . . to such an extent, that a fair and impartial jury
cannot be had to try the same in the said county." He asked
that the case be transferred to "the nearest county free from
these exceptions."[9] The gesture was dilatory and highly unusual because prosecutors rarely request changes of venue.
"This application for a change of venue on the part of the
territory, being so novel, and so unheard of in criminal practice, elicited great attention," an observer reported, "and
after a very able argument on the part of the Attorney General . . . the court would not consent, to establish a precedent
which . . . ran counter to the entire criminal practice of the
United States, and refused to grant the change of venue."[10]

Frustrated in these efforts, Ashurst tried to enter a *nolle
prosequi,* a legal maneuver to drop the prosecution yet allow
the matter to be brought up again, "but the attorneys for the
defense resisted this course . . . saying they could see nothing
in it but delay, vexation, and persecution."[11] On March 19,
Heath wrote Rynerson:

> I was not at all surprised at the unjust & oppressive course
> adopted by Ashurst; he is addicted to that style, I think.

The rulings of the Court were only such as I was prepared to expect, because I know they were just, and I should as soon expect to see the sun fall down as witness an unjust act on the part of Judge Brocchus.

Your course in resisting a nol. pros. was admirable. It was due to yourself & to your position as well as your friends. . . . I trust in a very few days to greet you here, rehabilitated in the just garb, which an honest jury such as I am sure you will have will assuredly throw around you.[12]

Choosing "an honest jury" proved to be difficult. After considerable haggling, the regular jurors list was exhausted and the court had to seek additional jurors before the trial could begin. Then the attorneys quarreled about the admissibility of the evidence of absent witnesses before the trial finally got under way. Ashurst seemed strangely subdued. Instead of pushing for a conviction for first degree murder, he asked the jury to return a verdict of murder in the fourth degree. A correspondent of the *New Mexican* suggested that Ashurst's conduct "shows what is rarely seen in prosecutors — a desire to do his whole duty but no more. He found upon a calm and dispassionate review of the evidence (where so much was at stake) — that he had been mistaken, and was manly and firm enough to correct that mistake."[13] Perhaps. But others believed that the attorney general — without key witnesses — was simply trying to salvage something out of a hopeless case.

The trial transcript apparently did not survive, and neither of the Santa Fe papers printed the testimony. None of the commentary on the trial provided any clue regarding the testimony presented. The *New Mexican*'s correspondent seemed more interested in Rynerson, who "bore himself as a patient gentleman of high intelligence, never murmuring under the delay and vexation that characterized his trial."[14]

When at length the attorneys had presented their cases,

Judge Brocchus delivered his charge to the jury. After first instructing the jury on the points of law, he declared:

> The jury . . . must carefully and dispassionately review all of the testimony in the case. They must remember the language used by the deceased toward the defendant the evening immediately preceeding the day on which the homicide occurred when, as it appears from the testimony, he, in a public place of resort, denounced the defendant as a d....d, seven footed son of a b...h, a thief and a coward.
>
> They will also remember the declaration made the same evening by the deceased, that he had been trying to pick a quarrel with the defendant but he, the defendant, would not take notice of it, and that he had a man rubbing up against him for that purpose, but that he could not succeed. They will also remember, that the witness to whom this declaration was made, testified that he immediately communicated it to the defendant, and warned him, the defendant, to beware of his personal safety.
>
> They will remember also, that the deceased on the forenoon of the day of his death, being Sunday, was at the Exchange Hotel, contrary to his usual custom, which was to go to church with his family; that the defendant boarded at that Hotel, and that the deceased remained there until the defendant, according to his usual habit, came in at or about dinner hour, when the fatal encounter took place. They will also remember, that both parties were armed with deadly weapons, and also the testimony as to the character of the deceased for violence of temper and conduct, and finally consider the bearing of each of the parties towards the other, at their final meeting, and all the circumstances and incidents of that sad occasion as represented by the testimony.

Following this discourse, Brocchus brazenly declared that "the court does not express any opinion to the jury, but simply desires to direct their attention to the prominent features of the evidence, in order to assist them in their efforts to reach a correct conclusion on the theory of justification, as set up in the argument for the defense." Having modestly disavowed any intention of directing a verdict, he added that

> the court feels constrained to advise the jury, that the high position occupied by the deceased . . . should not exercise any influence on their minds, in considering the question of the guilt or innocence of the accused. The life of the deceased was no more valuable or precious in the eye of the law, or the sight of Heaven, than that of the poorest and humblest member of society.

Brocchus concluded by informing the jurors that they had become

> judges both of the law and of the facts, as the court has the authority only in case of a conviction to set aside your verdict as contrary to the law and the evidence. The accused is entitled to the benefit of any reasonable doubt that the jury may, in view of the testimony, entertain as to his guilt.[15]

On March 22, 1868, William Logan Rynerson was acquitted. "Thus ends that matter," Heath wrote to a friend.[16] The *New Mexican*'s correspondent was more profuse, writing that Rynerson "now stands vindicated before the world, and his fair fame sacred from discredit and dishonor." Of Brocchus, he cooed, "he will be remembered as one of the kindest and most courteous gentlemen . . . and one of the ablest, fairest and best Judges that ever adorned the bench of New Mexico." The correspondent concluded, "We only hope that the Judge will be our next Chief Justice,"[17] and the paper's editors added, "We heartily concur in the verdict of the San Miguel jury."[18] The Santa Fe *Gazette* was more caustic:

Rynerson was put through the form of a trial in Las Vegas last week and was acquitted by the jury.

Comment is unnecessary.[19]

Comment may have been unnecessary for the *Gazette,* but the *New Mexican* took offense. The newspaper's editors challenged the *Gazette,* declaring that "the language carries with it something more than even a low criticism upon the court that tried Col. Rynerson, and we wish to know, what you wish to be understood by it. . . . Answer this."[20] The *Gazette* ignored the demand, for the moment.

With Rynerson freed at last, the Republicans intensified their effort to promote Brocchus to the chief justiceship. "The issue in the Rynerson case was as I had anticipated," Heath confided to Brocchus, "and your rulings upon the dilatory & other motions has added to your already established reputation among this people as a jurist, and an upright, just judge."[21] The *New Mexican* lavished Brocchus with praise, while the Republican leadership pressed his candidacy with their friends in Washington.

Confidence had returned to the Republican camp. "When I came here less than a year ago," Heath boasted, "there was no Republican organization in New Mexico. Politics ran mainly on men. Through my instrumentality, aided by a few loyal spirits, we organized a Republican Territorial Association & established the Grand Army here. The Legislature through an untiring zeal, was made & kept true to the Republican party."[22]

Heath now dropped all pretense regarding the governorship, stating flatly that "my appointment as Governor would be the severest blow that could be struck, such an appointment would lay the Collins-Mitchell party out like a corpse, whilst our party would rise like an eagle." But he warned that if he applied for the post, "I could not afford to be oversloughed for that appointment, particularly by my party.

. . . I should have but one recourse in such an event. Humiliated & politically disgraced, I should be inevitably forced out of the territory."[23]

Chaves was more practical. Clever still held the delegate's seat. Mitchell still sat in the governor's chair. And the appointment of John S. Watts to the chief justiceship appeared likely. Chaves kept the pressure on his friends in New Mexico to provide the proof he needed to confirm the 1867 election fraud, and he hung his hopes for the future on the Senate's conviction of Andrew Johnson. At the end of March, Heath reported to Chaves, "There is no news here. Everything is in *status quo*; we wait for *impeachment*. When that becomes *un fait accompli,* we shall hope for something beneficial to New Mexico and to our party."[24]

New Mexico's political wars had shifted to the halls of the U.S. Congress, with Chaves and Clever the strategists and primary combatants. As the apparent winner of the delegate contest, Clever had the advantage. Chaves now openly courted the Radicals while nervously prodding his New Mexico associates to accelerate their efforts to prove Democratic fraud in 1867, to provide the ammunition he needed to "kill the Kansas duck," as he derisively described Mitchell, and to work for the defeat of the Watts nomination for chief justice.[25]

Heath did his part, as best he could, bombarding Washington with letters against Clever, Mitchell, and Watts. "Watch Mitchell," he wrote to one of his contacts. "Do not let him play pig here & pup there."[26] Of Watts, he wrote to Senator James Harlan, "a more distasteful man to the party could not have been named by the President than this man is to us universally."[27] In letters to Senators Thayer and Lipton, he argued that "in the great & important struggle now going on between loyalty & disloyalty," the Senate could not afford to confirm a Copperhead appointed by Johnson even as that body considered impeachment of the president.[28]

But Clever skillfully maneuvered through the barrage,

not so much because he was right as because his enemies were vulnerable. As a delegate he largely ignored Chaves and concentrated his attack on Heath. Throughout the winter and spring, Clever's allies in New Mexico poured petition after petition against Heath into the offices of the secretary of state and attorney general, eventually obtaining — according to Clever — the signatures of "two-thirds of the citizens of New Mexico."[29] Early in March, Clever presented President Johnson with a catalogue of charges against Heath. Among his charges was the allegation that Heath had authored the resolutions against Slough. This "gross and scandalous libel upon the Judge" had led directly to Slough's death, Clever charged. Clever also submitted an affidavit from Don Jesus Maria Pacheco, the respected Republican senator from Taos, which provided, for the first time, real evidence of Heath's role as engineer of the Slough resolutions.[30]

After the legislature adjourned, Heath determined to go to Washington to help Chaves, but Mitchell, doubtlessly with Clever's aid, manipulated a three-month leave of his own that scuttled Heath's plans because both the governor and the secretary could not be absent from the territory at the same time. Heath protested to Washington and wrote a friend, "Mitchell has left for Washington on a leave granted upon false representations, & I anticipate his being ordered back."[31] He was wrong, and Mitchell was soon making the rounds in Washington with Clever.

Then came the first blow. Early in April, John S. Watts was appointed chief justice. "So Watts is appointed Chief Justice," Heath mused. "[H]e will not be confirmed in my opinion." But, Heath added hopefully, "impeachment goes on, and will be a success."[32] In May, the Senate failed to convict Andrew Johnson.

The heartened opposition used these developments to renew their assaults on Heath and Brocchus. In letters and editorials, John Slough's death haunted both men.[33] When

the *New Mexican* published a blistering editorial against
Chief Justice Watts and followed it with a spirited defense of
Judge Brocchus against the "eruptive venom" and "puerile
insinuations" of the *Gazette,* Russell and Collins turned their
editorial guns on Judge Brocchus as the henchman of Heath
and as a tool of the secretary in protecting Captain Rynerson
from conviction in the Slough killing.[34] Whatever could be
implied in what they had said before, the *Gazette*'s editors
now said explicitly, in the most virulent assault yet:

> In the Rynerson case he [Brocchus], from the time he began
> to mix in it, has violated the comities and outraged the
> proprieties of the bench. His whole conduct has shown that
> he was determined that Justice should be deprived of her
> dues, and that no punishment should be inflicted for the
> perpetration of the most horrid crime that was ever com-
> mitted in this community. His conduct in the *habeas corpus*
> investigation showed what the man was, what his determi-
> nation, and to what end he intended to bring the case in his
> court. The publication of his labored defense of the prisoner,
> called a decision of the court was a proclamation to the
> people that he, Perry E. Brocchus, Associate Justice, had
> taken charge of the case and that no harm should come to a
> single hair on the head of the immaculate Rynerson. His
> charge to the Jury, that was in the farce of a trial that took
> place in Las Vegas . . . shows how well and faithfully he
> adhered to the prisoner's cause to the end. Judge Brocchus
> sitting on the bench procured Rynerson's acquittal of the
> crimes for which he was indicted, and for which the moral
> sense of this community demanded he should be punished.
>   We do not charge that Brocchus was paid for his services
> in the case. We believe he was. We think he is not too good
> to receive pay. He showed himself as adept in the art of
> making acquittals easy and the inspiring cause may be
> readily imagined. Men of his character are always within
> the pale of suspicion. Off the Bench, he makes his living by
> his wits. On the Bench he is no better than he is off it. Not

a whit. A man who will bum in one position in life will bum in any other. A bummer will be a bummer, and Brocchus will be Brocchus whether he be in the Hotels of Washington City or on the Bench in New Mexico.[35]

This vicious attack elicited a response from the Santa Fe Bar association that praised Brocchus's "honesty and integrity of purpose" and protested against the *Gazette*'s "violently abusive article." The bar's "Card to the Public" was published in the *New Mexican* along with a brief editorial comment on the "villainous assault."[36] In response, the *Gazette* wondered why the bar had not defended Slough, Houghton, or Watts against equally intemperate charges by the *New Mexican* and concluded that the bar had done those gentlemen no disservice:

> Our conclusion then is that the bar have thought the characters of Judges Slough, Houghton, and Watts were of that sterner stuff which will bear public scrutiny and be improved rather than impaired by the criticisms of the press. But with the sensitive plant that has recently made its appearance among us it is different. He would not stand the test on his own merits, like the rest. His robe needed whitewashing and they who practice before his court and know his vanity and frailties, upon solicitation, whitewashed it for him.[37]

The *New Mexican* followed with a two-column editorial defending Brocchus from the charge that he had acted corruptly in the Rynerson case. After first praising the judge's legal analysis, the editors attacked:

> Unfortunately for the peace of society, the intense and bitter political animosities engendered by the late congressional election in this territory, associated themselves with the melancholy death of Judge Slough, and the Santa Fe

Gazette, closing its sight to the lessons of truth, evidence and reason, and yielding itself up to the spirit of a blind, bitter and fiendish partizan malevolence, has persistently aimed by the hue and cry of assassination and murder, to infuse into the popular heart the venom of its malignity toward Colonel Rynerson, and has with diabolical pertinacity, week after week and month after month, like the hungry hyena clamored for his blood.[38]

Ironically, Brocchus reacted to the criticism in much the same way that Slough had — although with more aplomb. Brocchus publicly threatened to beat John T. Russell, the editor of the *Gazette.* He made good on his threat a few days later when, while he was standing on the street talking with Merrill Ashurst, Russell stepped into the street a few feet away. Brocchus bowed to Ashurst, excused himself, approached Russell, and knocked the unsuspecting editor to the ground with two crashing blows. As friends carried Russell away, Brocchus calmly removed his gloves and tossed them into the street with the comment, "There, you've done dirty work enough."[39]

On May 2, the *Gazette* exposed Heath as the author of the removal resolutions, publishing the affidavit of Don Jesus Maria Pacheco, the man Heath had originally asked to sponsor the resolutions against Slough. In the affidavit, Pacheco swore that he "did not think it proper to take the responsibility of introducing" the resolutions and that he had passed them on to Rynerson, who subsequently introduced them to the council.[40]

The *Gazette* argued that Heath's role in the introduction of the resolutions explained why he had defended Rynerson so vigorously and why the *New Mexican* had been "so tenderfooted in all matters touching the guilt of Rynerson." Here, Russell declared, was "the propelling force" behind Heath's abuse of "all who would have seen justice done in the

Rynerson case."[41] The *New Mexican* responded that the authorship of the resolutions was unimportant and attacked "Poor Little Pacheco," labeling him a turncoat who "sold himself very cheap at last and the [C]opperheads are quite welcome to him."[42]

In June 1868, the beleaguered Chaves reported a rumor that Mitchell's friends were circulating a letter written by Heath to Jefferson Davis, asking for a commission in the Confederate army. "Of course such a thing I cannot believe," Chaves wrote.[43] But the rumor was all too real, and this time the evidence came crashing down on Heath. On June 15, Clever informed the President that Heath had violated his oath of office when he had sworn that he had "given no aid, countenance, counsel, or encouragement, to persons in armed hostility" to the United States because he had offered his services to Jefferson Davis and the Confederacy in 1861.[44] This astonishing charge was confirmed by John M. Schofield, the secretary of war, who transmitted a copy of a letter written by Heath to H. St. George Offutt of Montgomery, Alabama, dated April 9, 1861, which had been confiscated along with other documents at Richmond in 1865. The Bureau of Claims confirmed the facts.[45]

In the letter, Heath congratulated Offutt for securing a position in the "New Confederacy" and assured his friend that he "would have been there, where my heart ever is, had your President responded as promptly to me as my proffer of service was tendered to the new Government." He expressed his hope that he would yet hear from the Confederate president concerning his offer of services and went on to describe his credentials as a warm advocate of Southern rights. He declared himself to have been the first journalist "north of the Potomac" to have defended Southern principles, even though he was himself a Northerner. He swore that his sympathies had cost him "all I had in the world," and insisted that he would even then be in the South had he the means to support himself and his ailing wife.

He had sworn that he would be "one of your fellow citizens . . . if I am spared." Declaring that he believed a "collision" between North and South was inevitable, Heath had written, "There are tens of thousands of loyal hearts in the north who never will accede to coercion, and not only so, they will never pull a trigger against the south. Before I would march against my brothers of the south, I will suffer myself to be hanged on the first tree before the eyes of my own wife."[46]

The Santa Fe *Gazette* published the document without comment on July 11, allowing its impact to soak in for a week before editorializing on "That Letter." Then Russell could hardly contain himself. For months, Heath had railed against the disloyalty of the Democrats. Now Russell enjoyed the moment:

> No person could have committed himself more completely to the rebellion in its incipiency than did he. None could have expressed more admiration for the south and southern honor than he. None could have prayed more fervently for the success of the Confederacy than he did. None could have entertained greater feelings of animosity to the Union cause and northern men than he expressed. And none could have been more importunate for office under "our friend President Davis."[47]

Now, Russell declared, "His own record, as written by himself, has come home to roost and as he judged others so must he be judged."

The charges doubtlessly hurt Heath in Washington, where Mitchell was arguing the case of the opposition with members of Congress. Chaves confided to Heath that the Republican leaders in Congress were "utterly incapable of supporting and properly sustaining their party." He added, "I have never seen such a damned set of fools for partizans in my life."[48] Heath, now clearly fearful of his imminent removal, fired off an angry letter to Chaves, blaming him for failing to prevent the "unscrupulous and outrageous means" used by the opposition against him and generally complaining about Chaves's handling of affairs in Washington..

Chaves shot back a strongly worded epistle protesting against Heath's efforts to make him appear "derelict and negligent in not discovering their plans and thwarting them in their inception." He sharply reminded Heath that he had requested an explanation of the letter to Offutt. "I do not think it is fair for you to charge me with the delinquencies of the Republican party," he wrote. "They do not hold together. They do not always sustain their political friends notwithstanding most strenuous efforts in their behalf."[49] Heath enlisted the aid of Brocchus, who was then in Washington, against this "most diabolical attempt at my ruin." He claimed the Offutt letter was "the vilest forgery & calumny ever heaped upon a man." Brocchus dutifully protested to Secretary Seward, but he could do little else.[50]

In July, Watts was confirmed as chief justice of the Supreme Court of the Territory of New Mexico, much to the chagrin of the territory's Republicans, and his arrival in New Mexico set off a new round of controversies. Watts and Brocchus were old enemies, and their rancor soon erupted into an open feud. Within weeks, the two judges were at each other's throats. An important and politically charged case involving William Breeden, a Chaves insider and Republican kingpin, provided the stage. Breeden was a prominent attorney who had been indicted for having illegally obtained pension funds from a client. Watts had served as prosecutor when Breeden first appeared in court on a charge of perjury in the spring of 1868; Brocchus had been the presiding judge. Breeden had been acquitted.

Shortly after Watts became chief justice, Breeden was indicted for fraudulently securing pension monies from

James L. Collins. In this case, too, Breeden was acquitted before Judge Brocchus. Breeden was then indicted in the federal district court at Santa Fe on a related charge and was tried before Judge Houghton, who was holding court for Brocchus. He was convicted. He then moved for a new trial, which Houghton denied. When Houghton turned the court back to Brocchus, Brocchus heard Breeden's petition and granted a new trial, at which Breeden was acquitted.[51]

This astonishing scenario removed any doubt that the political environment had changed in New Mexico. Predictably, Judge Watts protested and demanded that Brocchus be removed from office. Predictably, the Democrats rushed to support Watts's allegations of misconduct. Predictably, Chaves, Heath, and the Republicans rushed to the defense of Brocchus — with one important defection. Stephen B. Elkins, who had so warmly endorsed Brocchus before, received information that Brocchus had obtained funds from Breeden's associates. Elkins thought that smacked of bribery, and he joined those calling for the removal of Brocchus.[52] When the legislature finally met in December, a new round of charges, investigations, and resolutions testified that little had changed in the year since John Slough died in the Exchange Hotel.

Senator Rynerson was in the thick on the new quarrel, which, ironically, centered on the territorial chief justice and the governor. The legislature had enacted a law that shifted the circuits of the territorial judges. Judge Watts was assigned to the Third Judicial District, which embraced most of southern New Mexico and was by far the most isolated district. The motives behind the shift were plainly political. Governor Mitchell vetoed the law, and Senator Rynerson introduced a series of resolutions criticizing Mitchell for his action.[53] New Mexico politicos were fighting over new names and new questions, but the invective and the motives were the same.

On February 20, 1869, Jose Francisco Chaves sent a tele-
graph to the editors of the *New Mexican:* "I have my seat."
Republicans rejoiced, but it was too little, too late.[54] Chaves
did his best for Brocchus and Heath, but he faced another
election in September that already dominated his thinking.
In February 1869, Heath and Mitchell became embroiled in
another quarrel over promised leaves of absence, and when
Mitchell prevailed, Heath assumed the role of acting governor of New Mexico, contending that Mitchell's "unauthorized" absence made him de facto governor until a new
appointment could be made.[55] Heath did not have long to
enjoy his illusion. When President Ulysses S. Grant assumed office, he decided to deal with the situation in New
Mexico by removing all of the federal appointees and start-
ing fresh. Mitchell, Watts, Brocchus, and Heath all lost their
positions.[56]

On April 9, 1869, the Senate confirmed the appointment
of Edward L. Perkins as secretary of New Mexico.[57] Ironically, even then Heath tried to wield power, demanding to
know if Mitchell should be recognized as governor when he
showed up in May.[58] With opinions from the Bureau of
Claims, both held their offices until their replacements arrived. For another full year, Heath kept matters in an uproar.

When William A. Pile, the new governor, first arrived in
Santa Fe in August 1869, he was initially impressed by
Heath, and he made a favorable report to President Grant in
October. Grant related his reservations about Heath, especially as they concerned the disposal of horses for Heath's
regiment at the end of the Civil War. Grant's comments
caused Pile some concern. In St. Louis, on his way back to
New Mexico, Pile met Heath's wife; she asked Pile to inter-
cede to save her husband's job. Pile told her that the matter
was hopeless, that Perkins was soon to take Heath's position.
Mrs. Heath then made several comments that led Pile to
believe that Perkins and Heath were manipulating the situa-

tion to save Heath's job in exchange for a payoff to Perkins.

This "corrupt bargain" soured Pile on Heath. When the legislature met in December, Heath created such a ruckus that Pile fired a terse telegram to Grant: "Need Secretary immediately. Heath embarrassing greatly. Perkins I fear corrupt collusion with him. Any honest capable man satisfactory." By that time, Pile's earlier positive report and Chaves's intervention on Heath's behalf had convinced Grant that he had misjudged Heath, and he had nominated Heath for the post of U.S. Marshal for New Mexico, a position held by John Pratt. When news of the nomination reached Santa Fe, reaction was instantaneous; even the Republicans were determined to be rid of Heath.

Stephen Elkins approached the new governor and urged him to sign a telegram to the chairman of the Senate Judiciary Committee to delay confirmation until reports from New Mexico could reach Washington. Pile agreed and affixed his signature to the telegram along with Elkins, Kirby Benedict, William Breeden, and a "hundred others." Heath was, the telegram said, "very objectionable." Puzzled by all of this maneuvering, Grant concluded that Pile was playing both sides of the fence and threatened to remove him. Pile hastily explained what had happened and saved his post. Heath's appointment was withdrawn, Marshal Pratt kept his job, and the crafty secretary was through in New Mexico.[59]

Yet, although hounded by the Offutt letter and largely disgraced in Republican circles, Heath returned to the territory long enough for one final embarrassment. A. P. Sullivan, the editor of the new Santa Fe *Post,* published a series of articles denouncing Heath as a coward, thief, and scoundrel. After reading one particularly intemperate article, Heath went looking for Sullivan. He found him in a downtown store and attacked him with a cane. Sullivan ran from the building with Heath firing a pistol after him.

Later that day Sullivan secured a revolver, marched up

the street to Heath's house, and opened fire on the former secretary as he stood on his porch. Heath returned the fire with a carbine. After both men had fired three times without effect, Sullivan turned and walked away. Marshal Pratt arrested both men, and the *New Mexican* printed a blistering editorial that reprimanded Heath for endangering the lives of innocent citizens: "Is there no remedy for wounded honor but in shooting holes through unoffending signboards and disturbing the peace of an entire community?" Heath's old friends now implored him, "In the name of common decency let us have done with it. 'Let us have peace.'"[60]

Not long after this incident, Heath left New Mexico for good. Eugene Ware claimed that Heath "became a refugee, fled to Peru, and died a pauper and a tramp [in 1874]."[61] Heath had hounded both Slough and Mitchell with charges of Copperheadism only to find his own career destroyed by evidence of his disloyalty. The *Gazette* had been right: He was judged by the same measure with which he had judged others.

With his political organization weakened at a critical juncture, Chaves lost his bid for reelection to Don Vincente Romero, who ran against Grant's "Peace Policy" toward the Indians.[62] Chaves and Breeden pulled the remnants of the party together and joined forces with Stephen B. Elkins and Elkins's young associate, Thomas Benton Catron, to forge the powerful political clique that came to be known — rightly or wrongly — as the "Santa Fe Ring." This combination would dominate New Mexico politics for years and baffle historians for more than a century. It would be a less frenetic and more efficient organization founded upon economic interests rather than the vagaries of party loyalty and family connections.[63] But the change did not eliminate the specter of violence.

On June 6, 1869, James L. Collins, the federal depositor, was found dead in his office, shot through the heart. His

William L. Rynerson, taken later in life. *Courtesy of New Mexico State University Library, Rio Grande Historical Collections.*

assailants had taken $100,000 from a safe, money that would have been used to pay troops stationed in New Mexico. A few days later, $65,000 of the stolen money was found stashed in a brewery next to the depository. Collins's killers were never identified or brought to justice.[64]

William Logan Rynerson, whose tenure as senator from Dona Ana County ended in February 1870, when he was appointed adjutant general for New Mexico, remained an active participant in Republican politics and became a prominent figure in the Santa Fe Ring. Always a controversial person, Rynerson was active both in political infighting and in money-making schemes.[65] In 1871, Dona Ana County was the scene of a particularly bitter election campaign. The usual charges and counter-charges flew between the Republicans and the Democrats, with Rynerson in the thick of the fight. During the campaign, Pablo Melendres, the probate judge of Dona Ana County, charged that his clerk, Ignacio Orrantia, had asked him to switch parties and to allow Orrantia to function as probate judge for a period of six days at election time to insure a Republican victory. Melendres claimed that he was offered Rynerson's job as customs inspector as a reward and that Orrantia said that Republicans were determined to win "whether they gained it by votes or use of bullets, clubs, rocks or blows." That seemed to be verified when relatives of the candidates for sheriff were fired upon by unknown assailants.[66]

On August 27, 1871, following rallies for both the Democrats and Republicans, the contending parties met on the plaza at Mesilla. When an exuberant citizen fired his pistol in the air, a riot erupted — leaving nine men dead and forty or fifty others wounded. One of the victims of the "Mesilla Riot" was John Lemon, the probate judge who had given Rynerson's opponent the certificate of election back in 1867.[67] Rynerson apparently was not involved in the riot, but he did run for Lemon's vacated post and later married Lemon's widow.[68] In September the Republicans, including Rynerson, were crushed in the elections.

Rynerson spent the next few years embroiled in litigation involving mining claims, land speculation, and land grant claims. Still, he remained a political insider and a popular local figure among both Hispanos and Anglos. In 1876, he was appointed district attorney for the Third Judicial District, which included Dona Ana, Lincoln, and Grant counties. This appointment involved him directly in the Lincoln County War. From the outset he was identified with the Murphy-Dolan faction, and his partisan use of his office certainly undermined the credibility of the courts and contributed to the climate of violence that resulted.[69]

For the rest of his life, Rynerson pursued a stormy course that in time brought him some financial success, if not the political victories he sought. He eventually joined forces with Colonel Albert Jennings Fountain, and the two of them even challenged the Santa Fe Ring in 1884 on behalf of southern New Mexico interests, in a bitter fight that divided the Republican party and sent a Democrat to Congress. Still, Rynerson remained active in Republican politics until his death on September 26, 1893, a successful rancher, lawyer, and entrepreneur.[70]

CHAPTER 6

Harvest of Violence

The Slough-Rynerson quarrel was a tragedy without heroes. When stripped bare of the rationalizations, homilies, and intrigues that overshadowed and rendered meaningless the evidence in the Slough-Rynerson quarrel, one simple, irrefutable fact survived: John Potts Slough died clutching at the pain in his belly while his political enemies gloated, and all the high-toned rhetoric and lofty principles of all the politicians in New Mexico could not hide the shame of it. John Slough's murder was a shoddy affair that should have provoked thoughtful reflection. It did not. The partisans scarcely blinked at the tragedy in their clamor to gain advantage from it.

The events that followed Slough's death revealed the malignant character of New Mexico politics even more clearly than did William Rynerson's act of violence. New Mexicans adjudged Rynerson guilty or innocent not according to the evidence against him but on the strength of their political loyalties. That reasonable men could so twist political "principles" demonstrated that the political climate of New Mexico tolerated — even encouraged — violence, and to the extent that the political leaders of both parties created and sustained that atmosphere, they shared William Rynerson's guilt. Despite the volume and the heat of their debate, Slough himself was not so much mourned as used.

But why?

The temptation is great to blame the bitterness of the

party struggles that began in New Mexico during the Civil War and Reconstruction. Doubtlessly, those years contributed conditions that heightened the potential for violence. But however much those troubled times exacerbated the partisan fight, the basic bargaining process had changed little. The struggle for political power, economic advantage, and cultural dominance merely moved into a new phase in response to the changing configuration of power at the national level. The war had raised the stakes, and the political convolutions that accompanied it heightened tensions. But after 1862, rhetorical debate had little to do with the great struggle being fought on the battlefields of the East. New Mexicans appropriated the language of the great conflict and postulated their loyalty. The war further destabilized economic and political affairs and invited demagoguery, but the real issues were closer to home. At stake was nothing less than control of the territory's future. The violence that followed the war was not the violence of frustrated masses of Hispanos yearning to be free of Anglo encroachments. That would come later, for in the 1860s evasion was the main tool of *los pobres*. Rather, the violence of the Reconstruction was within the governing classes themselves, among elites seeking political supremacy as the passkey to the exploitation of New Mexico's undeveloped resources.

John Slough's death was a critical link in a strain of political violence that would continue throughout the remainder of the nineteenth century. To some degree, Rynerson's success in avoiding conviction legitimized the tactic, which would be supplemented and sustained by more common forms of frontier violence — vigilantism, Indian uprisings, cattle rustling, and ethnic conflict — to give New Mexico an unenviable reputation. The political turmoil prepared the way for the bloody 1870s, when the Maxwell landgrant troubles, the Colfax County War, the Horrell War, the Tularosa Ditch War, and the Lincoln County War confirmed a violent connection to politics.[1]

In Colfax County, legal maneuverings over the Maxwell Land Grant erupted into violence in September of 1875, when the Reverend F. J. Tolby, a Methodist minister, was murdered. Tolby had been vocal in his criticism of members of the Santa Fe Ring for their efforts to control Colfax County and to manipulate events after Lucien Maxwell sold his grant to a group of investors. Actions taken by both the legislature and Governor Samuel B. Axtell appeared to confirm the suspicions of Colfax County citizens. Axtell's partisanship helped precipitate the "war," which included not only rumors of plots against such Ring opponents as William R. Morley and Frank Springer but also vigilante murders of persons suspected of killing Tolby, the use of troops, allegations that Thomas Catron and William Breeden had authorized Tolby's murder, and investigations into Axtell's conduct as governor.[2]

In the more notorious Lincoln County War, the involvement of the Santa Fe establishment was also evident — if not directly in the violence, then at least in protecting and justifying its partisans, on the one hand, while using the full power of territorial authority against its adversaries, on the other. Axtell was eventually removed from office; the reports of Frank Warner Angel, a special investigator sent from the departments of Justice and the Interior to investigate land-grant frauds in Colfax County, charges against Axtell and Catron, violence in Lincoln County, and the murder of John H. Tunstall, were filled with testimony to the complicity of territorial officials in the violence.[3]

Of course, much of the violence associated with the Colfax County War, the Lincoln County War, and other conflicts in the 1870s and 1880s was not directly related to the maneuverings of Santa Fe politicos, but these troubles were born of a pattern of action that promoted violence in ways that had political significance for the social system of the territory.[4] Politics, economic interests, and conflict were interrelated so thoroughly that violence achieved a kind of *de facto* legitimacy. Although much of the actual violence was played out among non-politicians, events were manipulated and used by the political elites in ruthless grasps for power and land.

The pattern continued into the 1880s. The American Valley murders of 1882–1883, the "accidental" shooting of William Morley in 1883, and the killing of Juan Patron in 1884 were all believed, by at least some New Mexicans, to have been politically motivated. And, as the decade came to close, rising activity by Hispano activists and *Las Gorras Blancas* (The White Caps) added to the turmoil. By the 1890s, political violence had become virtually an institution in the territory of New Mexico.[5]

On the night of November 7, 1888, a hidden assassin shot and killed Captain Dumas Provencher, a Democrat and an early settler in the Ojo del Gallo area, while he supervised the counting of votes as an election judge at San Rafael.[6] Early in 1890, a prominent Santa Fe Republican, Faustino Ortiz, disappeared. His body was found several months later on the outskirts of the city. In February 1891, J. Arturo Ancheta, a member of the territorial legislature, was shot and severely wounded while sitting in the offices of Thomas B. Catron, who was apparently the intended victim. In 1892, Sylvestre Gallegos, the chief of police in Santa Fe, was killed in a politically charged gunfight. Shortly thereafter, Francisco Chavez, a former sheriff of Santa Fe County (not to be confused with the former territorial delegate Jose Francisco Chaves), was ambushed and assassinated. Only days after Chavez's death, one of his allies, Juan Pablo Dominguez, died in a gunfight with the man he suspected of having killed Chavez. To make matters worse, the territorial capital at Santa Fe burned under suspicious circumstances, and a bitter campaign that autumn spread rumors of secret societies and assassination teams.[7]

When President Grover Cleveland appointed William T.

Thornton (ironically a law partner of Thomas Catron) to be governor of New Mexico, his intent was to end the political terrorism and outlawry in the territory. He had only minimal success. Early in 1894, assassins gunned down John Doherty, a former sheriff of Mora County.[8] Other murders occurred during those years, along with a series of violent incidents involving *Las Gorras Blancas,* labor unions like the Knights of Labor, the Penitentes (a secretive religious brotherhood), and outlaw gangs like that of Vincente Silva in the Las Vegas area, all of which had a disturbingly ethnic edge.[9] Beyond any doubt, a pattern of conspiratorial violence, consciously planned and implemented as political action, became a tool for dealing with the social and political issues of the time.

Political leaders of all political persuasions were accused of complicity in the violence. Thomas Catron and other Santa Fe Ring leaders were suspected of masterminding a string of killings from the Tolby murder in Colfax County to the Chavez assassination in Santa Fe. In 1896, Judge Albert Jennings Fountain and his son were murdered, and his probable killers were freed in one of the most patently political assassinations of the decade. Many people believed that Albert Bacon Fall, the leader of the resurgent Democrats, was the architect of the Fountain murders — and of others in the Tularosa area. The acquittal of Oliver Lee, who was tried for the Fountain murders, was orchestrated by powerful political interests.[10] On the evening of November 26, 1904, Jose Francisco Chaves was murdered at his cabin at Pinos Wells, near Cedar Vale in present-day Torrance County, as he sat before an open window, eating dinner. His killers were never caught, but the report was widely circulated that high officials in New Mexico were responsible.[11]

In 1908, Patrick Floyd Garrett, famous as the officer who tracked down Billy the Kid and as the man chosen, as sheriff of Dona Ana County, to investigate the Fountain murders, was gunned down beside the Las Cruces Road. Although

Garrett's murder was the result of personal and financial disputes, many New Mexicans believed that he was the victim of a conspiracy with at least some political roots. Clearly he had powerful enemies, and while the case was always controversial, the facts sustained a conspiracy theory sufficiently to convince James Madison Hervey, the New Mexico attorney general, and Captain Fred Fornhoff of the New Mexico Mounted Police that Garrett was the victim of a murder plot. Perhaps equally important, the conspiracy, if not overtly political, followed the pattern of political murders in previous years. In short, New Mexico politics provided the model, if not the motive. Notably, Fornhoff's report of the investigation disappeared from the files of the Mounted Police, leaving a large question mark about one of the most notorious murders in New Mexico.[12]

Although the research is inadequate, political murders seem to have subsided with statehood. The arrival of a more stable political order undermined the conditions conducive to assassinations in particular and to violence in general. Still, from time to time in the twentieth century, rumors of political violence have surfaced. A shadowy organization known as *La Mano Negra* (The Black Hand) allegedly operated in the Rio Arriba country in the 1920s and 1930s, and the sensational raid on the Rio Arriba County courthouse by Reies Tijerina and his followers in 1967 — although not involving political murder — at least kept alive the image of political violence in New Mexico.[13] But did the whole violent strain in New Mexico history from the arrival of Anglo-American traders to recent times represent a unique acceptance of assassination as a political tactic? And if it did, why did it happen there?

In some ways, of course, New Mexico's history mirrored national trends in the late nineteenth century to such a degree as to challenge the presumption that the territory's experience was anomalous. The period between the Civil War and World War I was an age of exploitation remembered as perhaps the most violent period in American history. It was the era of the last Indian wars, the violent suppression of black rights, the agony of labor strife, resurgent nativism, rampant vigilantism, range wars, feuds south and west, and agrarian unrest. Western gunfights and Southern "shoot-on-sight duels" were commonplace.[14]

Between 1865 and 1875, at least eight judges were assassinated nationwide. Half of them were killed in Louisiana. The others died in Georgia, Texas, New Mexico, and California. Of these, seven — including Slough — were killed in areas where Reconstruction or Reconstruction-related issues were prominent, under circumstances where the authority structure was weakened by public distrust, and in situations where emotions dominated reason in the political process.[15] Between 1865 and 1901, three U.S. presidents were assassinated, and in the census period between 1865 and 1874 alone, at least twenty-nine office-holders were killed or assaulted with the intent to kill, three-fourths of the incidents occurring in the Southern and the South-central states, including Texas. Indeed, on the strength of available statistics — which are notably incomplete — the South was more violent than any other region of the country. The unsettled conditions that accompanied the reconstruction of the war-torn South doubtlessly skewed the statistics, but the considerable migration of Texans into eastern New Mexico (an area still known as "Little Texas") and the role of Texans in the "wars" of the 1870s is worth noting.[16]

Still, the most striking — and least appreciated — feature of late-nineteenth-century American violence was that it *transcended* geography. The violence of the Gilded Age was not confined to western boom towns and unceded Indian lands, to an unreconstructed South, or to mills, mines, and city streets. Violence was a present reality for Americans in many discrete environments. A "root-hog-or-die" philosophy permeated politics, business enterprise, and race relations.

Corruption and "ring" politics characterized the period in virtually every region of the country. Materialism and *laissez faire* social attitudes blunted most reforms. Money and power were the driving forces of the land, and even violence could be justified in the name of progress and civilization, with most of the victims to blame for their unfortunate fates.[17]

Yet, taken together and set against the patterns of European development, broadly speaking, American violence was hardly exceptional. Capitalist modernization and expansion had provided the seedbed for conflict throughout Europe and its colonies, and the violence these forces spawned seemed always to center on industrialization, possession of the land, and the manipulation of natives, races, and classes that were out of harmony with the modernizing spirit. The United States was clearly in the throes of the painful transformation into a modern nation.[18]

The changes that overtook the nation in the aftermath of the Civil War were, if not distinctive, at least profound. Industrialization brought urbanization, with its negative payoff in crime, poverty, pollution, and corruption. Technology expedited the great migration to the cities, to the remaining unexploited regions of the South and Midwest, and to the new "frontiers" of the West. Those restless masses of people caught up in the social, political, and economic repercussions of change sought to find stability in the midst of new uncertainties. But mobility had its price. In new environments or environments transformed by the influx of workers or settlers or immigrants, a "boom phenomenon" unfolded, marked by floating populations of young, frequently unattached men and the gamblers, whores, saloonmen, and thugs who followed them to the "end of track," to mill towns, to cow towns, to mining camps, and to urban slums.[19]

The cold and impersonal materialism of the age fed a growing cynicism and a loss of personal identity among the alienated masses. The disruption of accepted norms and the resulting anger both roused the working classes and drove the new elites to defend their new-found power and wealth. Now the face of labor was not the Jeffersonian yeoman of former times nor even the self-sufficient workingman of the "free soil coalition" that had forged the Republican party in the 1850s, but an alien radical who joined Indians and blacks and Irishmen and Mexicans to constitute "the dangerous classes." Capital replaced labor as the source of all wealth in a new ideology that equated industrialization with civilization and justified the most extreme measures to remove obstacles to the new order.[20] And because progress was defined in terms of industrialization, the Indians, Hispanos, and Negroes, the urban poor, and the Southern poor whites — all those traditional groups in the modernizing world — could not be allowed to stand in its way.

These conditions did not provide the whole story of the Gilded Age — which had a progressive and creative face as well — but they did produce a preoccupation with violence, even in those places where violence was not epidemic. Personal violence was a favorite theme in the press of the day. Newspapers were filled with detailed accounts of murder trials and bizarre mayhem. Violence was romanticized in dime novels, and the public demonstrated a seemingly universal admiration for boldness and daring, even when displayed by desperadoes. Peace officers like Wild Bill Hickok were lionized, while Billy the Kid, Jesse James, and the Dalton gang were transformed into latter-day Robin Hoods.[21]

Contemporary observers attributed much of the violence to the effects of the Civil War, which had made killing and mayhem commonplace for hundreds of thousands of young men, infused them with the notion that violence was an acceptable way of dealing with problems, and fostered both a general cynicism about human life and an admiration for physical courage. Others saw the war as a mere excuse, observing that most of the war veterans had returned home and resumed normal lives without resorting to violence.

"Six out of eight of all the deliberate shooting affrays occur between men who were never in the army," declared a Wichita, Kansas, editor in 1875. He blamed the "trashy novels" and "dime editions" for "lending romance to lawlessness" and "giving charm to the character of the coward who has killed his ten or twenty men." He saw the greatest danger in "that numerous class of citizens" who idolized "the party who had killed his man," suggesting some connection between the violent fantasies of the penny dreadfuls and the real violence that led editors to write of the "manifest bloodthirstyness of the times."[22] Less than a year later, a San Antonio editor noted that Texas's newspapers were "lifting up their voices against the murder mania now raging in many parts" of the state. Considering Texas's reconstruction history, the editor's explanation was simple: "We have had bad government or no government for years, and have got used to it."[23]

Doubtlessly, the war did have its effects. At the very least, it left a nation of young men trained in the use of firearms against other men. Doubtlessly, too, it left a martial spirit and a rhetorical celebration of daring and physical courage in the general population, even though many of the war's veterans had grown cynical about such things. And, doubtlessly, in the devastated South and the divided border states, the residue of bitterness and the disruption of traditional norms and social controls created the seedbed of fresh violence.

Violent crimes doubled in the year following Appomattox. Many states witnessed alarming increases in criminal violence after the war; Kansas authorities reported in 1867 that 104 of 126 convicts in the state pentitentary were veterans, 60 of whom attributed their criminal behavior to "demoralization in the army." Following a tour of Ohio, Illinois, Michigan, and Kentucky, one observer reported that seventy-five percent of the recent admissions to prisons were men who had served in the army during the war, and a prison official in Massachusetts worried that many "young men who entered the service before they had learned a trade, and before their principles were firmly fixed," would fall "so readily into crime."[24]

Yet, the statistics could be misleading. With so many Americans under arms during the war years, not only were criminals more likely to be veterans after the war but military service may have actually reduced criminal behavior during the war. In any case, the majority of the war's soldiers did *not* enter lives of crime. Missouri, with its savage partisan struggle and a legacy of fraternal bitterness, experienced considerable post-war violence well into the 1870s, spawned a self-serving and cathartic literature about "retributive justice" and the honorable guerrilla, and produced a "dynasty of Western outlaws," beginning with the James-Younger gang; but even with their world demolished and their dearest assumptions shattered, most Missourians recovered the moral anchors that allowed them to make peace with their neighbors and to tether again the violent passions unleashed by the war.[25]

At the same time, the frontier myth, already venerable in 1865, fed the public's lust for sensationalism. The trappings of the frontier convinced most citizens that law and order ceased at the hundredth meridian. The violent realities of the war, the dislocations created by the new industrialism, and the perception of the West as a violent place fed a growing literature about violence. Historically, the frontier myth was a heroic saga in which violence was justified as regenerative in character. Reconstruction and the Gilded Age modified the myth into new forms that deplored the violence of the "dangerous classes" while justifying the violence of the elites who now dominated the new society.

The shift from an emphasis on the "dignity of labor" to a position that viewed working men as a dangerous proletariat was striking evidence of a new attitude that extended from the power elites to middle class businessmen.[26] In contrast, popular support for the James gang and the Daltons and even Billy the Kid derived in part from their choice of targets. Whatever the initial stimulus, modernization sustained conditions conducive to violence — cynicism, mobility, alienation, poverty, the boom phenomenon, nativism, and materialism — and resulted in a search for order that itself justified violence in defense of progress and "WASP" values.

At a personal level, nineteenth-century Americans shared surprising attitudes about violence. Central to the mindset of the times was the concept of honor. Much has been written about the militant South and the *code duello* and about the "code of the West," but violent self-redress in the face of insult or injury, real or imagined, was more characteristic of nineteenth-century life than has been generally recognized.[27] Moral standards were less pliable in the days before moral relativism and situational ethics. Courage and honor and manhood were standards central to the lives of Americans before the experiences of civil war and industrialization, which undermined the easy understanding of right and wrong.[28]

"Honor" implied character, magnanimity, courage, dependability, and the acceptance of other honorable men. Men went to great lengths to defend honor. The exact definition might vary from Victorian gentlemen's clubs to working-class saloons to bands of frontier bandits, but the code was genuine: A man's word was his bond, and to violate one's oath on even the simplest matter was to court disgrace and loss of face among his peers. Men had honor only when other men said so, and disrespect for women, coarse language, or cowardice could destroy it.[29] Honor could not be redeemed with persuasive arguments or by pleading innocence. Honor was restored through apology or some act of bravery, and in a surprisingly broad range of discrete environments, violence was the primary means of purging the shame.[30] In working-class urban neighborhoods, on Southern plantations, in Texas cattle country, in California mining camps, in military circles, among Irish work crews on the railroads, in outlaw gangs, and among politicians in many locales, honor was maintained by fist and knife and gun. Adherence to the proper masculine virtues could transform even bandits into heroes, particularly in areas like Missouri in the Reconstruction era and Oklahoma in the 1890s, where public confidence in the legal system was low.[31]

Honor was central to the Slough-Rynerson quarrel. One reason that politics was so volatile in New Mexico was that politicians and their supporters in the press constantly impugned their opposition's honor. The posturing and name-calling of the *New Mexican* and *Gazette* was more than yellow journalism. Assaulting the character of opposition leaders was the tactic Arny used against Benedict in 1863 before they joined forces. It was the tactic Republicans used against Slough that December of 1867, against Mitchell the following spring, and against Judge Houghton in 1869. It was the tactic the *Gazette* employed against Heath and Brocchus, even while its editors usually avoided direct attacks on Chaves, presumably because they still considered him a man of honor.

When Rynerson introduced the resolutions against John Slough in the Legislative Council, he did more than initiate a recall effort. The charges of drunkenness, profanity, and unfairness as a judge hammered Slough's sense of honor, and given his history of emotional outbursts at any criticism of his integrity or any insult to his person, his course was predictable, even inevitable. Similarly, Rynerson could not stand idly by once he had been called a coward, a dog, and a son of a bitch.

When the *New Mexican* tried to justify William Rynerson's act with the comment that "those who are best acquainted with far western life, properly understand that such language as Judge Slough used can be atoned only through

retraction and apology, or blood," the *Gazette* protested that
"our society does not justify any such conduct nor does it
palliate the crime of the shedder of human blood."[32] Paradox-
ically, both papers were partially correct. The *New Mexican's*
acceptance of violence deserved rebuke, but the *Gazette* ignored the plain fact that society *did* justify violence in affairs
of "honor." Judge Brocchus virtually exonerated Rynerson at
both the *habeas corpus* hearing and the trial on precisely that
ground.

Tied closely to the concept of honor was the right of self-
defense. As bizarre as the Brocchus decision seems after a
century, it was consistent in philosophy with a whole series of
nineteenth-century court decisions that eventually replaced
the English common law "duty to retreat" doctrine — which
required that a person retreat as far as possible before using
violence in self defense — with an Americanized doctrine of
self-defense tied closely to notions of honor.[33]

As early as 1830, in the case of *Grainger vs. State,* the
Tennessee Supreme Court, showing great concern for the
right of self-defense, denounced the "timid" and "cowardly"
behavior of a man who would not defend himself.[34] In 1839, in
a Kentucky murder case, the defense attorney proclaimed,
"When the rattlesnake gives warning of his fatal purpose, the
wary traveler waits not for the poisonous blow, but plants
upon the head his armed heel, and crushes out, at once his
venom and his strength." In rhetoric strikingly like that used
to free Rynerson, the attorney averred, "Sirs, there are sins
against individuals, as well as sins against heaven, which
can only be expiated by blood — and the law of Kentucky is
that the man who is attempted to be *cowhided,* not only *may,*
but *must,* if by any possibility he can, *at the time,* kill the man
who attempts thus to degrade him." This "law," the defense
attorney proclaimed, transcended the legal statutes of Kentucky. It was "the law of Kentucky instinct."[35]

Both Slough and Rynerson understood that law. Rynerson

was himself a Kentuckian who came to New Mexico by way of the mining camps of California. Slough was a veteran of "Bleeding Kansas" and the Colorado mining towns. Both men were veterans of the Civil War and accustomed to violence, and both men knew they lived in a territory where virtually every man carried a gun. Both understood the honor code, a code that held, as the courts held in Texas, that a man had no duty to retreat farther than "the air at his back."[36] Nor was the doctrine confined to the frontier. In 1875, the Ohio Supreme Court held that a "true man" was "not obliged to fly" in the face of an assault. The following year, the Indiana Supreme Court dismissed the duty-to-retreat doctrine with the pronouncement that "the tendency of the American mind seems to be very strongly against the enforcement of any rule which requires a person to flee when assailed."[37]

In neighboring Arizona, when Justice of the Peace Wells Spicer set the Earp brothers and Doc Holliday free in the killing of the McLaury brothers and Billy Clanton following a preliminary hearing in 1881, he declared that the Earps had seen "the dire necessity of giving the first shot to save themselves from certain death."[38] As late as 1921, the "Texas rule" was tested before the United States Supreme Court in the case of Brown vs. United States. No less a jurist than Oliver Wendell Holmes declared "that if a man reasonably believes that he is in immediate danger of death or grievous bodily harm from his assailant he may stand his ground and that if he kills him he has not exceeded the bounds of lawful self-defense."[39]

These notions of honor and self-defense formed the basis for the conduct of both of the principals in the Slough-Rynerson quarrel as well as the essence of the arguments with which Rynerson's conduct was justified. But beyond these personal justifications, New Mexicans appealed to another venerable canard in American life. Throughout U.S. history, men have accepted violence when they conceived it to be in the interest of the community. Basically honest men joined lynch mobs in the South, rode with vigilantes on successive frontiers, and destroyed Indian villages because they believed they were defending the interests of the community. Moreover, the justifications of violence have differed little whether the subject was Sand Creek or My Lai, the lynching of a black man in Georgia or the hanging of a horse thief in Kansas. In cotton patch and cow town, the pattern has been the same.[40]

This familiar appeal was evident in the rhetoric of both the *New Mexican* and the *Gazette,* and, indeed, in the correspondence of the principal players in the Slough-Rynerson tragedy. The distrust and fear was so great that both the nominal Democrats and the nominal Republicans saw each other not simply as the opposition but as a sinister force that had to be destroyed, root and branch. John Slough was not merely an unpopular judge whose partisanship deserved rebuke; in the minds of those who opposed him, he threatened the very future of the territory as they envisioned it. That the threat was more imagined than real never really mattered. Once Slough was perceived as a threat, any measure that would secure his removal could be justified or excused. If his enemies stopped short of condoning violence — and not all of them did — they still were pleased at the net result.

"Although it is not good to be [glad] over the misfortune of others," Manuel Romero of Sapello, an ally of Jose Francisco Chaves, wrote to his friend Aniceto Salazar following Slough's murder, "the notice you give me of the death of the Chief Justice, does not fail to rejoice me greatly, because there has come to his end an enemy of our party, of high rank, which is a great triumph for us, and a great loss for them, and we may say, as folks say, 'the less of a bad thing the better.' " Romero then added a remarkable appeal for more violence, calling upon his party "to pitch into this nest of Jews" and "give them blazes until the devil gets them. War!!! War with them!!!" He specifically mentioned "that assassin," Don Jesus Maria Baca y Salazar, the militia commander, and suggested that he should not be allowed to "go about smiling, nor walk at his pleasure about the streets of the capitol [*sic*] of the Territory."[41]

Clearly, then, both Slough's murder specifically, and political violence in New Mexico generally, fell within the broad patterns of American violence. Slough's murder might well be explained in terms of one or more of these themes, and yet factors distinctive to New Mexico contributed significantly to the climate of anomie that existed there in the last decades of the nineteenth century. The peculiar politics of mistrust was perhaps the central factor. Although ethnic in origin, the tenuous and unstable- modus vivendi achieved a life of its own, more notable for factional volatility than for ethnic animosity. Had the arrangement represented a clear Hispano-Anglo dichotomy, the politics would have been more predictable and less treacherous. Instead, the division of power — with Anglos dominating federal offices and Hispanos controlling the legislature — demanded accommodations across ethnic lines that amounted to arrangements of convenience and interest rather than of principle.

But the larger problem for the political system was that shared democratic principles had never taken root. The Anglo-American legislative system imposed by the Anglo-American settlers was implemented largely by Hispanic legislators who were able to give a continental flavor to the law and politics of New Mexico. In the long run, the *modus vivendi* actually eased the transition to a truly intercultural politics that incorporated elements important to both Hispanos and Anglos and gave Hispanos a central role in politics, which differed qualitatively from the less satisfactory situations in Texas, Arizona, and California where *Mexicanos* either were largely excluded from the political process during the formative years or were exploited more overtly along class and ethnic lines.[42]

The single most important political fact of New Mexico history that differentiated New Mexico from other states in the Southwest was that Hispanos constituted a majority of the voters in New Mexico throughout the nineteenth century. The percentage of Hispanos was — and remains — significantly greater in New Mexico than in any other state. Nowhere else did *Mexicanos* have sufficient clout to dominate the legislature and thus to protect Hispanic social and economic interests. New Mexico's natives faced Anglo-Saxon racism as surely as the natives of other Southwestern territories and states, but their political position assured them influence in the circles of power.

In practice, of course, the arrangement brought few benefits to the masses of Mexican-Americans, since it was based upon an "old boy" arrangement between Anglo political and economic interests and the *ricos* who controlled *los pobres* through the *patron* system. The system worked mainly because of the *laissez faire* attitudes of *los pobres* to the territorial government. As long as their traditional ways were secure, they were satisfied. Nevertheless, the potential threat of all those Hispanic votes was a potent force in the power games, and the native leaders were able to use that reality to avoid Anglo domination. Rivalries among the traditional family factions added another volatile factor. Clearly, Hispanos were quite capable of defending their interests and of reminding the Anglo elites just how fragile their control really was.[43]

One critical factor in the equation was the political geography of New Mexico. With the Hispanic population concentrated in the center of the territory, along the Rio Grande northward from Albuquerque in an area offering the fewest attractions to Anglos, the politicians were able to work out arrangements that allowed Anglos to pursue their economic plans without disturbing the traditional world of *los pobres* in the territory's population center. The *ricos* delivered votes to the Republican party, and the party protected their interests in return. Republican control of this region was critical to the emergence of the Santa Fe Ring and to Republican domination of territorial politics.

Notably, the Maxwell land-grant troubles, the Colfax County War, the Lincoln County War, and most other lesser conflicts over land and economic development took place outside of New Mexico's Hispano-dominated counties, generally east of the mountains. Although some of these areas had substantial *Mexicano* populations, they were not part of the Republican stronghold. Only when the land-grant schemers chose targets within the Hispano-dominated counties (as they did in San Miguel County in the 1880s) did *los pobres* arise from their apparent apathy. Then they moved — both at the ballot box and in societies like *Las Gorras Blancas*. Each time the Republicans were reminded of their dependence on Hispano votes, they scurried to mend fences.

The political convulsions of New Mexico were never neatly divided along class and ethnic lines. The Lincoln County War, for example, was certainly not ethnic in nature (although there were issues of particular interest to Hispanos involved), nor was it a class conflict, since not only the small ranchers and laborers who acted as partisans but also the social and economic elites were divided between the Murphy and McSween factions.[44] Still, when it served their purposes, politicians sought to make issues appear to be based on ethnic differences. Governor LeBaron Bradford Prince's statement that New Mexico's situation should "not be judged by American standards, as if the people were intelligent Anglo-Saxons," placed blame for the Santa Fe murders of the 1890s on groups of radicalized or criminalized Hispanos from lower socio-economic levels. The rationalization served the establishment stereotype of the "dangerous classes," but it simply did not wash, either in the hands of contemporary establishment observers like Prince or in the works of their apologists.[45]

In the short run, the *modus vivendi* nurtured an angry, mean-spirited suspicion that so permeated the system with conspiratorial and self-interested motivations that politics became an ugly process of defaming and villifying party leaders. Again, the conflict itself was not so much ethnic as factional, not so much issue-oriented as interest-bound. The unstable nature of the factional alignments produced confusion in the decision-making processes — confusion that manifested itself in bitter personal rivalries. Squabbles were multilayered: between Santa Fe and Albuquerque and Las Vegas, between political leaders for party control, between government appointees and locals, between the old Hispano family parties. The strident, almost hysterical attacks on party leaders were invitations to violence, and when the attacks occurred in an environment already destabilized by Indian wars, civil war, ethnic rivalries, isolation, and frontier conditions, assassination could not be far behind.[46]

The rise of *Mexicano* resistance to establishment domination in the 1890s as represented in the activities of *Las Gorras Blancas* and *El Partido del Pueblo Unido* (The United People's Party) reflected a clarification of the issues between the New Mexico establishment and *los pobres* at precisely the moment that political assassination became most commonplace.[47] Yet, ironically, the first had little apparent connection to the last. *Mexicano* resistance was a measured response to the age-old questions of land and culture, to issues where the political order impinged on traditional values and immediate questions of economic and social survival. The assassinations of the same period, in contrast, were not ethnic in any definable way, and, in fact, were linked directly to the legacy of partisan politics of the establishment itself. *Las Gorras Blan-*

cas escalated one conflict to new levels with new clarity. The assassinations represented the convulsions of a political establishment corrupted by decades of conflict and intrigue. *Mexicano* defense of land and water rights and of other vital interests constituted a separate, although related, kind of political violence from the institutional violence associated with establishment politics.[48]

Still, the radical politics of *Las Gorras Blancas* and the Knights of Labor may well have intensified the violent mood of the 1890s simply because it represented a direct challenge to politics as usual in New Mexico. As a threat to the *modus vivendi,* radical groups jeopardized traditional relationships and defined sharply ethnic and class divisions at odds with the status quo. When the editor of *La Voz del Pueblo* declared in 1892 that the main issue in New Mexico was "not one of political parties, but one of honest people against monopolies and their gang of paid assassins," he was challenging not only the Republican party and the Santa Fe Ring but also the basic assumptions of power politics in New Mexico.[49]

Doubtlessly, then, the new pressures intensified the existing political rivalries and bred new suspicions. The Republican leadership attempted to link the Democrats to the Knights of Labor and *Las Gorras Blancas* and to blame the violence on "very ignorant and excitable" Mexican-Americans, while radical spokesmen accused the Republicans of manipulating gullible Hispanos to do their dirty work of assassination.[50] Yet the Ancheta shooting was almost certainly an attempt to kill Thomas Catron, with some indications that prominent Democrats, including Sheriff Chavez, were involved, and the weight of evidence left little doubt that Chavez died because he threatened to revive the sagging fortunes of the Democrats or that Republicans in high places were parties to the conspiracy. The trial of the Borrego brothers for the Chavez murder and allegations concerning the role of Thomas Catron in the affair unmasked the hypocrisy of the system and checked the excesses of both Republican and Democratic power brokers, at least for a time. Such moments prevented anarchy and validated the rule of law, but they did not wholly eliminate the specter of political murder.[51]

Throughout the territorial period, personality played an especially large role in the political wars. The politics of personality made public differences of opinion into matters of private and personal dispute. "Different from any country I have ever been in, a difference between men in Politics, or political views, in New Mexico furnishes the best basis for personal animosities," Herman Heath wrote shortly after Slough's death. "National politics here have, heretofore, had no place. Hence, party policy & party action have been based solely upon *personal* grounds — political personalism."[52] Heath may well have touched on the central factor in the death of John Slough as well as a perceptive understanding of New Mexico politics. Fifteen years later, Governor Prince would lament, "It is the curse of this country that political prejudices run so high."[53]

The pattern of violence in New Mexico was a crazy quilt of diverse elements, but, taken together, the various factors have a graphic unity. Violence is the product of condition, rather than of place.[54] The peculiar history of New Mexico sustained the kind of unsettled conditions that encouraged violence over a surprisingly long time. The ecology of violence there was ultimately the product not merely of an ethnic conflict that pitted Hispanos against Anglos but of a broad-based cultural confusion that created a fundamental systemic frustration.

New Mexico's history throughout the nineteenth century was anomalous. In no other place did traditional Hispanic political and social values survive the onslaught of the nation's Manifest Destiny so tenaciously. Isolation, the unique political system it produced, and the internecine war with Navajos, Apaches, and Comanches predisposed the territory toward violence, but the critical factor in sustaining favorable conditions for violence appears to have been the inability of federal authorities to establish a political solution that could resolve the cultural differences or, more importantly, defuse the politics of personality.[55]

Violence most often occurs in situations where the authority structure is insufficient or where confidence in the authority structure has been undermined by inefficiency or loss of credibility.[56] But in New Mexico the problem was that the new authority structure, represented by the United States government and its agents, was unable to displace entirely the old, localistic authority structure of the native New Mexicans. In the central quest for power and stability, New Mexico could find few unifying values and little common ground, but struggled instead with a *modus vivendi* that satisfied no one and denied the territory a true party system.

The resulting confusion, with its overlays of suspicion, fraud, intimidation, and corruption, weakened support for U.S. institutions and undermined confidence in critical territorial offices. Neither governors nor courts nor legislature could unclog the logjam of values. Arny's bold plan to make the Republican party the dominant force in New Mexico politics was tacit recognition of the need for change, but even his designs were forced to accommodate the existing arrangement. With the close of the Civil War, expanding American capitalism and the forces of modernization gradually closed in on New Mexico, adding new pressures and new players, and politics in that cynical and materialistic age found a kind of order not in a viable two-party system based upon shared values but in the phenomenon of ring politics. But ring politics by definition was manipulative and corrupt even when it was effective, so that the potential for violence was sustained.

Without any doubt, the most violent period of New Mexico's stormy political history came between Reconstruction and statehood. For nearly forty years beginning with the murder of John Slough and ending with the ambush of Jose Francisco Chaves, political violence was institutionalized in New Mexico. Violence was an acceptable weapon in a war between parties, not unlike the fratricidal conflicts of the Middle East.[57] Assassination was condoned and encouraged by Republicans and Democrats alike. But again, why? The peculiar vagaries of Reconstruction politics were hardly enough to explain the murderous politics thereafter even within the broader context of territorial history. New Mexico's political wars paralleled several important developments.

First, the territory's violence began during the initial efforts to create and sustain organized and disciplined political parties, and it did not subside until the emergence of a viable, modern (albeit distinctive) two-party system in the first decade of the twentieth century. Despite considerable advantages for Republicans, practical realities in New Mexico created a politics of equilibrium that did not change significantly until the 1930s. Miguel Otero's appointment as governor weakened the old system, giving the governor broad-based support among Hispanos and greatly enhancing the political importance of the governorship. As a Hispano native who also had credibility among Anglos, Otero exercised authority as no previous governor had been able to exercise it. Factions and coalitions remained a leading characteristic of the party battles, but the modernization of party organization rendered violence less acceptable — and less necessary — as a political tactic. Otero became an important symbol of ethnic fusion and helped to foster a new attitude of cooperation that modified the old politics in New Mexico. Notably, his tenure as governor, 1897–1906, paralleled the decline of political violence and assassination in the territory.[58]

Second, the violent years paralleled New Mexico's battle

for statehood. Slough's murder occurred during a hiatus of statehood activity that lasted through the Reconstruction era, but New Mexico's uncommonly long territorial period underscored certain realities that contributed to the strain of violence. For one thing, residents remained genuinely divided over the merits of statehood. Some were anxious for the kind of home rule that statehood would bring; others feared that statehood would mean higher taxes, the loss of patronage, and subordination to entrenched political groups. Cultural differences loomed large in the debate, both within New Mexico and at the national level. Opponents of statehood frequently employed racist stereotypes about Hispanos to explain violence and disorder.

Notwithstanding the essential ethnocentrism that motivated much of the opposition to statehood, the focus was the old issue of the Americanization of New Mexico and the threat that change presented to the *modus vivendi* established during the 1850s. Only with the Americanization of New Mexico's economy and the arrival of a significant Anglo-American population did statehood occur, and only with the reformulation of the accommodation between the factions that accepted both American legal institutions and Hispanic traditions did violence subside.[59] The ethnic difficulties in neighboring Arizona (which had a similarly long territorial period and came into the Union the same year as New Mexico), like those in Colorado, California, and even Texas, operated more as a "minority problem" within a system created and controlled by Anglo-Americans from the beginning.[60]

Third, violence remained a constant reality because the legal system was so politicized. John Slough's crusade for judicial reform did not derive from a mean-spirited contempt for New Mexican custom and usage but from a determination to put the judicial house in order. The simple truth was that every element of the territory's judicial process, from arrest to sentencing, was tainted with politics. Jurors were willing partners in a system that treated the administration of justice in terms of political affiliation. In 1869, when President Grant removed the entire New Mexico judiciary, he did so in part because of the deplorable reputation of the courts. By 1876, when Henry L. Waldo was appointed chief justice, New Mexico literally faced a reign of terror.

Criminal assaults and murders were so commonplace even in Santa Fe that citizens were paralyzed with fear. In a period of a few weeks in the summer of 1876, two men fought a gun battle in the plaza at Santa Fe, spraying bullets during the busiest part of the day; four young thugs kicked and beat to death Dr. J. P. Courtier, an aged and crippled citizen who lived near the plaza; and a drunken youth, firing his pistol into the air, killed a young woman. Judge Waldo, in convening court at Santa Fe in July of that year, lashed out at the situation in a stirring charge to the Grand Jury:

> Assassination after assassination has been occurring with startling frequency and rapidity; shootings and cuttings take place around us with the most impudent and outrageous defiance of law; one of our wisest and most valuable statutes, that against the carrying of deadly weapons in settlements and plazas . . . is violated daily and hourly and in numberless instances. Yet in all these cases there is scarcely a conviction had or a penalty inflicted; or if so the punishment imposed by weak and loose-minded jurors, has not been at all commensurate with the enormity of the offenses.[61]

Judge Waldo explained that this state of affairs existed "because the laws are not enforced. Because there is a total failure in the performance of their duty by those who are required to aid in executing the laws! An entire want of efficiency in the adminstration of justice in this Territory! Crime witnesses the failure of justice and plumes itself upon

an almost absolute immunity from punishment."[62] His indictment of affairs was not exaggerated. When two of the youths
who had brutally murdered Dr. Courtier were brought to trial
and convicted, the jury specified that the defendants be sentenced to one year in the county jail.

Similar decisions in other cases prompted the *New Mexican* to declare that the situation "brings prominently into
view the utter failure or rather farce of trial by jury as it
obtains in New Mexico."[63] In the sensational Colfax County
trial of the Reverend Oscar P. McMains for complicity in the
lynching of one Cruz Vega (who had allegedly confessed
under torture that he had murdered the Reverend Tolby, a
friend of McMains), McMains was found guilty of murder in
the fifth degree and was fined three hundred dollars. That
verdict was set aside on a technicality, and at a second trial
the charges were dismissed.[64]

And so the system struggled along. The activities of William Rynerson during the Lincoln County War as a partisan
of the Murphy-Dolan faction, the confused state of law enforcement there, and the competition between local justices
and constables and the territorial courts and sheriffs guaranteed a disrespect for law and a fundamental partisanship
among jurors.[65] Contempt for the law was deepened by the
belief, well-founded, that politics was the main basis for conviction and sentencing.[66] New Mexico's old practices died
slowly; in the interim, all too frequently, at places like
Socorro, Albuquerque, and Las Vegas, men sought justice at
the mouth of a revolver or in the finality of new rope. And
judges alone could not change the system.

Here, too, some similarities of experience existed between
New Mexico and other parts of the Southwest, but despite
periodic corruption and occasional outbursts of violence elsewhere, New Mexico remained distinctive. Arizona's history
was surprisingly free of political violence, if not of ring politics. Even in the Earp-Clanton troubles of 1881–1882, which

some thought had political overtones, the political parties rapidly condemned the Cochise County violence that was clearly rooted in more personal causes.[67] Violence in Texas was more Southern in flavor, more closely tied to the Reconstruction, long-standing feuds, and race — all of which sometimes had political overtones.[68] Violence elsewhere — in California and in Colorado, for example — was linked to other causes. While judicial indiscretions, lynching bees, political corruption, and disrespect for the law existed throughout the Southwest at one time or another, nowhere outside New Mexico did violence become so directly linked with the political order.[69]

Fourth, the violent epoch in New Mexico paralleled its economic modernization. The hidden agenda in the manipulations of Chaves and Heath and Mitchell and Clever was the development of New Mexico's economic opportunities. The machinations of the Santa Fe Ring and its opposition throughout the years reflected a contest among nascent entrepreneurs over a wide range of economic interests. The land-grant struggles, the Lincoln County War, and even the growing militancy of *los pobres* in the 1890s owed much to economic interests. Indeed, the social and economic conflicts over control of land and resources largely defined the political agenda throughout the territorial years. New Mexico's reputation for violence and negative stereotypes of the native population also delayed both political and economic progress. The coming of the railroad, establishment of direct connections to Eastern business interests, and the population growth that accompanied economic change forced a new order.[70]

Initially, economic diversity intensified violence, since the Santa Fe Ring could not singularly control the expanding multiplicity of interests. In response, the battle to establish political supremacy among the factions ushered in the particularly bloody period that lasted from 1888 to 1904. Issues as varied as the tariff, free silver, and conservation broadened the economic perspective of New Mexico. But if modernization initially disrupted the economic, political, and social establishment in sometimes violent convolutions, in the long run it moderated and sanitized the instruments of policy. As early as April 1892, Governor Prince pointed out the impact of the railroad and economic change when he advised the Secretary of the Interior that "rule by coercion, threats and 'bulldozing,' " was under attack. "[C]onditions have changed and modern and American systems are needed," Prince wrote, adding, "The native people will not stand what they did 15 years ago. The new population will not stand it at all."[71] A reputation for lawlessness and disorder did not attract investors, and more conventional political weapons replaced the gun and the knife.

On balance, then, New Mexico's peculiar history sustained conditions conducive to violence over an extraordinarily long period of time. The conditions themselves were hardly unique; they were in fact the kind of conditions that encourage violence everywhere. The thing which perpetuated the violence after 1846 was an institutionalized compromise that delayed a real resolution of differences and created a political order that subverted both traditional Hispanic practices and Anglo-American law. The result was a world of interest politics maintained by federal patronage and economic advantage, a world where the legal order lacked real legitimacy, and a world where the authority structure was so personalized that competition for control and legitimacy allowed violence to become a functional instrument of policy.[72]

If ever a man was the victim of time and place, it was John Slough. He stepped into a political situation for which he was wholly unprepared. Never a partisan in the conventional sense, he probably never understood the politics of New Mexico even though he was eventually drawn into its web. Slough's passion in the territory was judicial reform. His conduct on the bench was justified by the standards he brought with him, and he was honest and straightforward in everything he did. But he was also combative and insensitive to his cultural surroundings. Slough's obstinate, dogmatic approach and his uncontrollable temper not only alienated many people but also prevented him from developing warm supporters who might have agreed with his goals. Even more fundamentally, his self-ordained mission to impose the forms and spirit of Anglo-American law upon the people of New Mexico challenged the reality of institutional and behavioral norms in the territory. Even if his rulings were correct technically, he mistook legality for legitimacy.[73]

If Slough's personality had been different, if his commitment to his crusade for legal reform had been less fervent, or if he had properly understood the political environment, he might have survived. Instead, he became to the Republicans who opposed him a symbol of a potentially oppressive force in New Mexico, a force that ran counter to the public good as they understood it. Accustomed to the lax practices of the past, *los pobres* saw in Slough an Anglo tyrant, local authorities saw in him a threat to the status quo, and Republican politicians saw in him a threat to the *modus vivendi* that was the key to the consolidation of power in the Republican party. John Slough was more dangerous than Robert Mitchell or James L. Collins or Charles Clever because he was not a politician and cared little for the games that sustained the system. Mitchell and the others at least played the game. Slough was oblivious to it.

No evidence ever emerged that Slough was the victim of a clandestine murder plot, but he certainly was the victim of a political conspiracy. His enemies had recognized and then exploited his weaknesses, provoking an outburst that would unknowingly become an alibi and a justification for his murder — and all because he threatened their strategy for political control of New Mexico. Slough's rage seemed to both validate the charges contained in the resolutions against him and provide an excuse for his murder. William Rynerson probably acted alone, driven by his own sense of honor (which was not unlike Slough's) and his loyalty to his mentors. He had gone to the Exchange Hotel that December day in 1867 determined to kill Chief Justice Slough.

And he did. But Rynerson's act was not merely personal. He was, after all, a political outsider, a newcomer seeking access to the inner circle of the Republican elite, when he killed Judge Slough. His quarrel with Slough grew out of overtly political activities, and even if the tall man from Las Cruces acted because of personal animus against the obstreperous judge, his crime became enmeshed in the fundamental power issues of the day. The Republican response to the homicide alone transformed Slough's death into a basic move in the bargaining process of New Mexico politics. That they benefited from his demise, however briefly, ameliorated the crime and validated the tactic. Rynerson was not only vindicated, he was politically rewarded. The lesson of the Slough-Rynerson quarrel lay there.

Notes

Abbreviations in Notes

AGO   Adjutant General's Office
AGP   Attorney General's Papers
APDJ   Appointment Papers, Department of Justice
ARW   *Arizona and the West*
CMSR   Compiled Military Service Record
DJ   Department of Justice
DRMN   Denver *Daily Rocky Mountain News*
GLR   Gary L. Roberts
GPO   Government Printing Office
JAH   *Journal of American History*
KHC   *Kansas Historical Collections*
LALJ   Letters of Application, Lincoln and Johnson
LR   Letters Received
MMWH   *Montana, the Magazine of Western History*
MVHR   *Mississippi Valley Historical Review*
NA   National Archives
NMHR   *New Mexico Historical Review*
NMSRCA   New Mexico State Records Center and Archives
NMTP   New Mexico Territorial Papers
RG   Record Group
SCZL   Special Collections, Zimmerman Library
SFNM   Santa Fe *New Mexican*
SFWG   Santa Fe *Weekly Gazette*
UNM   University of New Mexico
USAC   United States Army Commands
WDNI   Washington *Daily National Intelligencer*
WHQ   *Western Historical Quarterly*

Prologue

1. This reference requires a qualifier. At the turn of the century, William A. Dunning of Columbia University and his students documented the corruption of the Reconstruction period so prodigiously that they fixed the view of the carpetbaggers as a pack of scoundrels who looted the South for their own profit. See William A. Dunning, *Reconstruction, Political and Economic* (New York: Harper & Row, 1962), originally published in 1907. The Dunning stereotype prevailed for decades but has since been dispelled. For a more balanced view, demonstrating that many carpetbaggers were honorable and capable men, see Richard Nelson Current, *Those Terrible Carpetbaggers: A Reinterpretation* (New York: Oxford University Press, 1988), and Eric Foner, *Reconstruction: America's Unfinished Revolution, 1863–1877* (New York: Harper & Row, 1988). The same is true of New Mexico, but revisionist history notwithstanding, enough shoddy opportunists did exist to explain the origin of the stereotype.

2. Kenneth N. Owens, "Patterns and Structure in Western Territorial Politics," WHQ, I (1970): 373–392; and Vincent G. Tegeder, "Lincoln and the Territorial Patronage: The Ascendancy of the Radicals in the West," MVHR, XXXV (1948): 77–90, provide useful analyses. Eugene H. Berwanger, *The West and Reconstruction* (Urbana: University of Illinois Press, 1981), *passim,* is especially helpful in assessing the impact of Reconstruction on territorial politics.

3. Reconstruction in New Mexico has not been treated definitively. The most useful items are two articles by Lawrence R. Murphy, "Reconstruction in New Mexico," NMHR, XLIII (1968): 99–115; and "William F.M. Arny: Secretary of New Mexico, 1862–1867," ARW, VIII (1966): 323–338. Murphy's book, *Frontier Crusader — William F.M. Arny* (Tucson: University of Arizona Press, 1972), 115–134, treats the party battles after 1867 only lightly. Also helpful are Howard Roberts Lamar, *The Far Southwest, 1846–1912: A Territorial History* (New Haven: Yale University Press, 1967), 134–138; Robert W. Larson, *New Mexico's Quest for Statehood* (Albuquerque: University of New Mexico Press, 1968), 92–94; and Porter A. Stratton, *The Territorial Press of New Mexico* (Albuquerque: University of New Mexico Press, 1969), 84–85.

4. See especially Richard Maxwell Brown, "Historical Patterns of Violence in America," *Violence in America: Historical and Comparative Perspectives.* 2 vols., edited by Hugh Davis Graham and Ted Robert Gurr (Washington: GPO, 1969), 1: 43–45; James F. Kirkham, Sheldon G. Levy, and William J. Crotty, *Assassination and Political Violence: A Report to the National Commission on the Causes and Prevention of Violence* (Washington: GPO, 1969), 38–40; Warren A. Beck, *New Mexico: A History of Four Centuries* (Norman: University of Oklahoma Press, 1962), 172–173; William J. Crotty, "Assassinations and their Interpretation within the American Context," *Assassinations and the Political Order,* edited by William J. Crotty (New York: Harper & Row, 1971), 25–26; and Lamar, *Far Southwest,* 192–195.

5. Brown, "Patterns of Violence," 44–45. Brown's analysis is reprinted in his classic *Strain of Violence: Historical Studies of American Violence and Vigilantism* (New York: Oxford University Press, 1975), 14–15. See also Beck, *New Mexico,* 173.

6. Lamar, *Far Southwest,* 37–38.

7. The literature is voluminous. For a representative sample, see Jack Forbes, *Apache, Navajo, and Spaniard* (Norman: University of Oklahoma Press, 1960); Frank McNitt, *Navajo Wars: Military Campaigns, Slave Raids and Reprisals* (Albuquerque: University of New Mexico Press, 1972); William A. Keleher, *Turmoil in New Mexico, 1846–1868* (Albuquerque: University of New Mexico Press, 1986); Edward H. Spicer, *Cycles of Conquest: The Impact of Spain, Mexico, and the United States on the Indians of the Southwest, 1533–1960* (Tucson: University of Arizona Press, 1962); Dan L. Thrapp, *The Conquest of Apacheria* (Norman: University of Oklahoma Press, 1967); and Charles L. Kenner, *A History of New Mexican–Plains Indian Relations* (Norman: University of Oklahoma Press, 1969).

8. L. R. Bailey, *Indian Slave Trade in the Southwest: A Study of Slave-Taking and the Traffic of Indian Captives* (Los Angeles: Westernlore Press, 1966), *passim;* Robert J. Rosenbaum, *Mexicano Resistance in the Southwest: "The Sacred Right of Self Preservation"* (Austin: University of Texas Press, 1981), 3–27.

9. Lamar, *Far Southwest,* 23–27; Rosenbaum, *Mexicano Resistance,* 20–27. See also Paul Horgan, *The Great River: The Rio Grande in North American History,* vol. 1 (New York: Holt, Rinehart & Winston, 1954), 389.

10. Elizabeth A.H. St. John, *Storms Brewed in Other Men's Worlds: The Confrontation of Indians, Spanish, and French in the Southwest, 1540–1795* (College Station: Texas A & M University Press, 1975), 98–154; Forbes, *Apache, Navajo, and Spaniard,* 200–280. See also Charles W. Hackett, *Revolt of the Pueblo Indians of New Mexico and Otermin's Attempted Reconquest, 1680–1682* (Albuquerque: University of New Mexico Press, 1942); Oakah L. Jones, Jr., *Pueblo Warriors & Spanish Conquest* (Norman: University of Oklahoma Press, 1966); and J. Manuel Espinosa, *Crusaders of the Rio Grande* (Chicago: Institute of Jesuit History, 1942).

11. Janet Lecompte, *Rebellion in Rio Arriba, 1837* (Albuquerque: University of New Mexico Press, 1985); David J. Weber, *The Mexican Frontier, 1821–1846: The American Southwest Under Mexico* (Albuquerque: University of New Mexico Press, 1982), 261–265; Jacqueline Dorgan Meketa, *Legacy of Honor: The Life of Rafael Chacon, A Nineteenth Century New Mexican* (Albuquerque: University of New Mexico Press, 1986), 21–40; Lynn L. Perrigo, *The American Southwest: Its People and Cultures* (New York: Holt, Rinehart & Winston, 1971), 150–152.

12. Lamar, *Far Southwest,* 53; David Lavender, *Bent's Fort* (New York: Doubleday, 1954), 202; Charles R. McClure, "The Texan–Santa Fe Expedition," NMHR, XXXXVIII (1973): 45–56.

13. Marc Simmons, *Murder on the Santa Fe Trail: An International Incident, 1843* (El Paso: Texas Western Press, 1986); Lamar, *Far Southwest,* 53–54.

14. Lavender, *Bent's Fort,* 283–284.

15. *Ibid.,* 302–318; Lamar, *Far Southwest,* 68–69.

16. Lamar, *Far Southwest,* 101. Tensions were so high that in 1849 Joab Houghton and Richard H. Weightman fought a duel, fortunately without fatal result for either man.

17. *Ibid.,* 36–82.

18. *Ibid.,* 27–34, 60–61, 70–82; Larson, *Quest for Statehood,* 13–75; Rosenbaum, *Mexicano Resistance,* 25–26.

19. Robert W. Larson, "Territorial Politics and Cultural Impact," NMHR, 60 (1985): 251; Rosenbaum, *Mexicano Resistance,* 14–15, 25–27.

20. Lamar, *Far Southwest,* 28–29, 84–87; Rosenbaum, *Mexicano Resistance,* 25–26.

21. Victor Westphall, *Thomas Benton Catron and His Era* (Tucson: University of Arizona Press, 1973), 24.

22. Lamar, *Far Southwest,* 84–86, 94–105; Larson, *Quest for Statehood,* 25–74.

23. Lamar, *Far Southwest,* 87–88, 106–108.

24. *Ibid.,* 73, 84–85.

25. Kirkham, et al., *Assassination and Political Violence,* 5, 163, provided critical theoretical ideas for this analysis. G. L. Seligmann, "Withdrawal: A *Mexicano* Response to Anglo Intrusion in 19th Century New Mexico," an unpublished draft of a study in progress, 3–8, also helped shape the interpretation presented here. Seligmann argues persuasively that native New Mexicans were neither apathetic nor powerless. Rather, he suggests, the majority of the common people pursued the course of "withdrawal." He points out that while the *ricos* became "very adept practitioners of the new system," the common people were indifferent to the new political order so long as it did not intrude on traditional ways or the important issues of land and water.
    These conclusions differ in tone from other analyses. Jack E. Holmes, *Politics in New Mexico* (Albuquerque: University of New Mexico Press, 1967), 29–31, speaks instead of a "prompt and efficient accommodation to a new political system," arguing that Hispano and Anglo cultures "shared more basic conceptions than they disputed." Ultimately, he says, "The emerging system made crucial adjustments with a minimum of strain." William J. Parrish, "The German Jew and the Commercial Revolution in Territorial New Mexico, 1850–1900," NMHR, XXXV (1960): 1–23, 129–141, also describes the "reasonably peaceful convergence of New Mexico's three cultures and other ethnic groups." Rosenbaum, *Mexicano Resistance,* 25–27, 186–187, appears to agree, although his position is not explicit and his study generally seems to support a conflict model. Larson, "Territorial Politics," 262–268, challenges accommodation in favor of conflict in terms that may well include the *modus vivendi* described herein. Rosenbaum and Larson together produced "Mexicano Resistance to Expropriation of Grant Lands in New Mexico," *Land, Water, and Culture: New Perspectives on Hispanic Land Grants,* edited by Charles L. Briggs and John R. Van Ness (Albuquerque: University of New Mexico Press, 1987), 269–310, in which they agree that "the competing factions involved did not divide neatly along Anglo-Mexicano lines."
    Two considerations are noteworthy in trying to resolve the apparent differences. First, the contention here is that while the ethnic differences provided the seedbed of the dispute, the conflict was not purely ethnic — a conclusion that might square with Holmes and Parrish and certainly does support Rosenbaum and Larson in their collaborative conclusions. Second, as Larson, "Territorial Politics," 263, notes, "intercultural relations in territorial New Mexico were more harmonious than in other parts of the Spanish-speaking Southwest" — probably because of the Hispano influence in the legislature

— but that fact would not preclude a systemic frustration, rooted in the cultural differences, which manifested itself not in a flagrantly Hispano-Anglo conflict but in a mutant politics. In fact, the evasion of the system by *los pobres,* what Seligmann calls "withdrawal," helps to resolve the apparent differences in interpretation. Ultimately, some explanation must be provided for a level of political violence in New Mexico that simply did not exist in other areas of the Southwest where general levels of violence were equally high. See Brown, *Strain of Violence,* 15.

Chapter 1

1. Henry Connelly was a Virginian by birth, a medical doctor by training. He emigrated to New Mexico by way of Kentucky and Missouri and was an early arrival in New Mexico with the Santa Fe trade. He lived in Chihuahua for a time before settling permanently in New Mexico. In 1849 he married the widow of Don Mariano Chavez and moved into a large house at Los Pinos in Valencia County. He did not practice medicine, except in rare emergencies, but instead became active in business and politics. No adequate biographical treatment exists. See Keleher, *Turmoil in New Mexico,* 122–123. Calvin A. Horn's sketch in *New Mexico's Troubled Years: The Story of the Early Territorial Governors* (Albuquerque: Horn & Wallace, 1963), is inadequate.

2. Ray C. Colton, *Civil War in the Western Territories* (Norman: University of Oklahoma Press, 1959), 59–69; Ralph Emerson Twitchell, *Old Santa Fe* (Chicago: Rio Grande Press, 1963), 380–384; Martin H. Hall, *Sibley's New Mexico Campaign* (Austin: University of Texas Press, 1960), *passim;* David Westphall, "The Battle of Glorieta Pass: Its Importance in the Civil War," NMHR, XLIV (1969): 137–154; Gary L. Roberts, "Sand Creek: Tragedy and Symbol." Unpublished Ph.D. Dissertation (Norman: University of Oklahoma, 1984), 122–129.

3. Murphy, "Arny," 336–337. Useful insights are found in Darlis A. Miller, "Hispanos in the Civil War in New Mexico: A Reconstruction," NMHR, 54 (1979): 105–123; and William I. Waldrip, "New Mexico During the Civil War," NMHR, XXVIII (1953): 163–182.

4. Gerald Thompson, *The Army and the Navajo: The Bosque Redondo Reservation Experiment, 1863–1868* (Tucson: University of Arizona Press, 1976), 10–27; Aurora Hunt, *Major General James H. Carleton, 1814–1873: Western Frontier Dragoon* (Glendale: Arthur H. Clark Co., 1958); Clifford E. Trafzer, *The Kit Carson Campaign: The Last Great Navajo War* (Norman: University of Oklahoma Press, 1982); Lawrence C. Kelly, *Navajo Roundup* (Boulder, Colorado: Pruett Press, 1970).

5. Lamar, *Far Southwest,* 124–126. Seligmann, "Withdrawal," 8–10, points out that despite the French-born Lamy's leading role, he was essentially an outsider himself who did not understand the *Mexicano,* as was revealed in his quarrel with Father Antonio Jose Martinez.

6. Thompson, *Army and Navajo,* 84–99.

7. Murphy, "Arny," 329–336.

8. Lamar, *Far Southwest*, 126–128.

9. Thompson, *Army and Navajo*, 100–122.

10. Murphy, "Arny," 335; Lamar, *Far Southwest*, 126–128; Aurora Hunt, *Kirby Benedict: Frontier Judge* (Glendale: Arthur H. Clark Co., 1961).

11. Murphy, "Arny," 336–337.

12. Interestingly, no biography exists of Chaves, who led the kind of full and exciting life that would make good history. Keleher's brief sketch in *Turmoil in New Mexico*, 480–481, still offers the best introduction. Other sources include Ralph E. Twitchell, *Leading Facts of New Mexican History*, new edition, vol. 2 (Albuquerque: Horn & Wallace, 1963), 400–401; and Paul A.F. Walter, Frank W. Clancy, and M. A. Otero, *Colonel Jose Francisco Chaves, 1833–1904* (Santa Fe: Historical Society of New Mexico Papers, 1926).

13. Keleher, *Turmoil in New Mexico*, 480–481.

14. *Ibid.* Chaves's military service is mentioned in Meketa, *Legacy of Honor*, 223–275.

15. Berwanger, *West and Reconstruction*, 90, 187. Apparently, as Berwanger notes, Chaves was so influential with Johnson that others enlisted his help in patronage matters, as in the case of Allen Bradford, who sought Chaves's support in his bid for the governorship of Colorado.

16. Murphy, "Arny," 337.

17. Arny to William H. Seward, January 6, 1865, New Mexico Territorial Papers, Department of State, NA, RG 59.

18. Murphy, *Frontier Crusader*, 132.

19. Horn's account of Mitchell's governorship in *Troubled Years*, 115–133, is, at best, a superficial review of his term. Background material is provided in "Sketch of the Career of General Robert B. Mitchell," La Cygne (Kan.) *Weekly Journal*, April 26, May 3, 1895, reprinted in KHC, 1923–1925, XVI (Topeka: Kansas State Historical Society, 1925), 632–637; Wendell H. Stephenson, "Robert Byington Mitchell," *Dictionary of American Biography*, vol. 7, edited by Dumas Malone (New York: Charles Schribner's Sons); Twitchell, *Leading Facts*, 2: 410–411, 336n; and Eugene F. Ware, *The Indian War of 1864*, edited by Clyde C. Walton, Bison Edition (Lincoln: University of Nebraska Press, 1960), 105–106, 450–451. Ware, who served under Mitchell and was apparently one of his favorites, said of him, "He looked like a king. He was an exceedingly handsome man, with a full, dark-brown curly beard and mustache." See also Jane C. Sanchez, "'agitated, personal, and unsound . . .'" NMHR, XLI (1966): 217.

20. Ezra J. Warner, *Generals in Blue* (Baton Rouge: Louisiana State University Press, 1964), 453–454; *Notices of the House of Representatives of the State of Ohio in the Fifty-Second General Assembly, Convened January 7th, 1856.* (Columbus, Ohio, n.p., 1857), 33.

21. Cincinnati *Enquirer*, September 13, 1856, quoted in the Cincinnati (Ohio) *Gazette*, February 16, 1857; Columbus (Ohio) *Gazette*, January 16, 1857; "Jeffersonian" to the Editor, January 21, 22, and 23, 1857; Cincinnati *Gazette*, January 22, 23, and 24, 1857; and *Journal of the House of Representatives of*

the State of Ohio, Being the Second Session of the Fifty-Second General Assembly Commencing on Monday, January 5, 1857 (Columbus: Statesman Steam Press, 1857), 58–59, 70–71.

22. *Journal of the House,* January 22, 1857, 58–59; Jeffersonian to Editor, January 22, 1857, Cincinnati *Gazette;* Cleveland *Leader,* January 19, 1857.

23. Jeffersonian to Editor, January 30, 1857, Cincinnati *Gazette.* Corry, who had been absent from the House at the time of the incident because he had smallpox, and Slough had some personal difficulty between them that predated the controversy. Democratic newspapers accused Corry of taking advantage of Slough's difficulty to settle the score. See the *Ohio Statesman* quoted in the Cincinnati *Gazette,* January 31, 1857.

24. Columbus *Gazette,* January 30, 1857; *Journal of the House,* January 29, 1857, 99.

25. Cincinnati *Gazette,* February 2, 4, 5, 6, 7, 9, 10, 11, 12, 13, 16, 17, 18, 19, 20, 25, 27, 1857.

26. Jeffersonian to Editor, January 30, 1857, *Ibid.,* February 2.

27. Statement of Mr. Yaple in Cincinnati *Gazette,* February 7, 1857.

28. Cincinnati *Gazette,* February 2, 1857.

29. Address of William M. Corry on February 12, 1857, in *Ibid.,* February 13. See also the Cleveland *Leader,* February 18, 1857, (Denver) *Daily Rocky Mountain News,* "Clarendon" to Editor, December 24, 1867, and Cincinnati *Commercial,* December 29, 1867.

30. Cleveland *Leader,* November 9, 1857; Slough to John A. Halderman, December 7, 1857, and January 3, 1858, John A. Halderman Collection, Kansas State Historical Society; Rosa M. Perdue, "The Sources of the Constitution of Kansas," KHC, vol. 7 (Topeka: Kansas State Historical Society, 1902), 136n; Cincinnati *Commercial,* December 29, 1867; John P. Slough to the attorney general, January 6, 1866, Appointment Papers for New Mexico, Department of Justice, NA, RG 60.

31. Ovando J. Hollister, *Boldly They Rode: A History of the First Colorado Regiment of Volunteers* (Lakewood, Colorado: The Golden Press, 1949), 47.

32. Roberts, "Sand Creek," 112–129, *passim.*

33. *Ibid.,* 129, 134; Hollister, *Boldly They Rode,* 74, 86. Arthur A. Wright, "Colonel John P. Slough and the New Mexico Campaign," *Colorado Magazine,* XXXIX (1962): 100–105, argues that Slough resigned because he feared court-martial for disobeying his orders to remain at Fort Union rather than advancing to Glorieta. Slough himself confided to Samuel F. Tappan his fears of assassination. See Slough to Tappan, February 6, 1863, Letters and Other Manuscript Materials Written by J. M. Chivington, S. F. Tappan, L. N. Tappan, J. P. Slough, E. W. Wynkoop, et al., between the Years 1861 and 1869, Microfilm copy at the Colorado Historical Society, Denver.

34. Hollister, *Boldly They Rode,* 86.

35. Roberts, "Sand Creek," 130–131.

36. Warner, *Generals in Blue,* 453; Bruce Catton to GLR, October 18, 1965; Otto

Eisenschiml, *The Celebrated Case of Fitz-John Porter: An American Dreyfus Affair* (Indianapolis, 1950), 80–81. Eisenschiml suggests that Slough's loyalty to the Union had been questioned at the outset of the war. More certain is that Slough's role in the Fitz-John Porter case reveals that he, along with others on the court, sought to please Secretary Stanton.

37. Slough to Edwin M. Stanton, December 31, 1864, LR, General File, AGO, 2694-S-1864, NA, RG 94; Hiram Pitt Bennet to Slough, January 30, 1865, Western Americana Collection, Yale University Library; Slough to Seward, June 3, 1865, William H. Seward Papers, University of Rochester Library, Rochester, New York; John Evans to Slough, June 14, 1865, William H. Gilpin Collection, Chicago Historical Society; Slough to Andrew Johnson, August 7, 1865, LALJ, 1861–1868, M-60, Roll 55, NA, RG 59. See Roberts, "Sand Creek," 458–459, 467–468, 505, 507–508, for discussion of these events.

38. WDNI, April 20, 21, 22, 1865.

39. Joseph Hooker to Henry Halleck, June 25, 1863, General's Papers, AGO.

40. L. Palmer to John G. Parke, May 19, 1865; "Charges and Specifications against John P. Slough, Brig. Genl., U.S. Vols & Military Governor of Alexandria, Va., General's Papers, AGO.

41. Slough to Stanton, June 8, 1865, General's Papers, AGO.

42. DRMN, July 31, August 1, 3, 1865.

43. Slough to Johnson, August 7, 1865, LALJ. Slough initially had no luck in finding a position. He appealed to the Governor of Ohio for assistance, but the governor, after assuring him of his "disposition" to help him, added "but I feel that nothing that I could do, would aid you in the way you indicate." He also noted, "For reasons that to me are quite sufficient . . . I have, as a rule, declined to make such recommendations to the administration." Also Charles Anderson to Slough, December 7, 1865, Cincinnati Historical Society, Cincinnati, Ohio. Papers in the appointment files in Washington support that Slough had attempted to enlist Anderson's aid in securing the chief justiceship. His letter to the attorney general included endorsements from H. E. Paine, a congressman from Wisconsin; Samuel C. Pomeroy, senator from Kansas; Benjamin Franklin Wade, senator from Ohio; General James B. Steedman; Rutherford B. Hayes, congressman from Ohio and future president; and Jerome B. Chaffee of Colorado. See LALJ.

44. Arie Poldervaart, *Black-Robed Justice* (Santa Fe: Historical Society of New Mexico, 1949), 69–70; Murphy, *Frontier Crusader,* 132. Slough's commission as chief justice of the Supreme Court of New Mexico is dated January 26, 1866, "Commissions of Judges," 2: 207, General Records of the Department of State, NA, RG 59. Slough's official "Territorial Oath of Office and Allegiance," dated March 14, 1866, along with handwritten oaths signed by Slough and witnessed by Kirby Benedict, late chief justice; William L. Gwynne, clerk of the first judicial district; and Joab Houghton, associate justice, are filed along with a letter from Slough to the attorney general, March 17, 1866, in the "Federal Courts File," AGP, General Records, DJ, NA, RG 60.

45. Slough to the attorney general, January 6, 1866, APDJ.

46. Slough to Stanton, August 17, 1866, John P. Slough CMSR, S-179c, AGO.

47. In May 1866 Slough took leave for the purpose of moving his family to New Mexico. See Slough to the attorney general, April 23, May 14, 1866, AGP. In the summer of 1866, Kirby Benedict organized an expedition to the gold fields on the Gila River. John Slough, along with his colleague on the bench, Joab Houghton, District Attorney Charles P. Clever, John Greiner (the receiver at the U.S. depository), and other territorial officials accompanied Benedict. They departed on July 20, 1866, and the newspapers reported their return on November 2, 1866. See Hunt, *Benedict,* 191. Slough was also active in promoting mining interests. See SFWG, October 5, 1867; SFNM, November 5, 1867.

48. Poldervaart, *Black-Robed Justice,* chapter 2; Rosenbaum, *Mexicano Resistance,* 25–26.

49. Poldervaart, *Black-Robed Justice,* 62–64; 70; Hunt, *Benedict,* 170–190.

50. Twitchell, *Leading Facts,* 2: 398–399.

51. The petition was dated September 27, 1866. A printed copy was enclosed in the Letter of Jose Francisco Chaves to Henry L. Dawes, March 26, 1869, Chaves Folder, APDJ.

52. Arny to Seward, September 26, 1866, NMTP.

53. SFNM, September 13, 1866.

54. Murphy, "Reconstruction," 100–104; Horn, *Troubled Years,* 118.

55. Murphy, *Frontier Crusader,* 132–133. Much correspondence relating to this conflict is found in the Letterbook of William F.M. Arny, William G. Ritch Collection, Henry E. Huntington Library and Art Gallery, San Marino, California. See also the extensive correspondence in NMTP.

56. Horn, *Troubled Years,* 119–120. See also Clever's *Opinion . . . upon the Question "Whether or not, the Hon. W.F.M. Arny is by law the Secretary of New Mexico at this time" Given to the House of Representatives,* dated December 20, 1866, NMTP.

57. The best source on Heath's career is the Bureau of Claims Report entitled "Case of H. H. Heath Secretary of the Territory of New Mexico," dated June 30, 1868, NMTP, which details Heath's career from his birth in New York through his difficulties in New Mexico. See also Heath to H. St. George Offutt, April 9, 1861, NMTP.

58. See Herman H. Heath, CMSR, First Iowa Cavalry, for details of Heath's early military service.

59. Heath, CMSR, Seventh Iowa Cavalry, AGO; Ware, *Indian War of 1864,* 435–436.

60. Ware, *Indian War of 1864,* 11, 96, 435–436; J. Schofield to William H. Seward, June 26, 1868, and Heath to H. St. George Offutt, April 9, 1861, Bureau of Claims Report, June 30, 1868, NMTP. See also Heath's CMSR for the Seventh Iowa Cavalry, AGO; and SFWG, October 12 and November 9, 1867, for references to his dismissal from the army for "speculating in government property" and his subsequent reinstatement and honorable discharge.

61. Berwanger, *West and Reconstruction,* 94–97. See the quote from the letter of A. C. Dodge and Charles Mason in "Abstract of Correspondence in Opposition to H. H. Heath," June 1868, NMTP.

62. *Ibid.;* Chaves to Johnson, December 29, 1866, NMTP.

63. General Order No. 65, June 22, 1867, Heath CMSR, Seventh Iowa Cavalry, AGO.

64. Quoted in the Leavenworth *Conservative,* April 26, 1867, and reprinted in the SFWG, January 25, 1868.

65. Heath's course of action is revealed most clearly in Heath's Letterbook for 1867–1868, which the author examined at the office of the late Senator Clinton P. Anderson in Washington, D.C., in 1972. Since that time the Letterbook has been deposited in SCZL, the University of New Mexico, Albuquerque. A series of letters written by Chaves to Heath during the same period provides a unique opportunity to see the interchange between the two men. The Chaves letters are housed at the Arizona Historical Society in Tucson.

Chapter 2

1. Arny to Mitchell, January 7, 1867, Arny Letterbook. Arny's letter was a blistering response to a report that Mitchell had accused Arny of stirring up the controversy against Slough for political reasons. Arny was furious at Mitchell's attitude, demanded to know if he were correctly reported, and protested that his only interest was New Mexico's well-being. In his letter he called Slough "your *professed friend! Judge Slough!!!*" in obvious derision. Truthfully, the Republicans had never been happy with Slough because he had unseated Benedict. At the time of Slough's appointment, several attempts were made to retain Benedict, which involved some rather prominent national Republicans. See Chaves to James Speed, attorney general, January 6, 1866; Lyman Trumbull and Richard Yates to Andrew Johnson, January 10, 1866; and David Davis to Johnson, January 18, 1866, Benedict File, APDJ.

2. *Tomas Heredia vs. Jose Maria Garcia, habeas corpus* appeal, Supreme Court for the Territory of New Mexico, published in the SFWG, February 2, 1867.

3. Berwanger, *West and Reconstruction,* 28–30; Murphy, "Reconstruction," 99–103, 112n; Lamar, *Far Southwest,* 89,131.

4. Murphy, "Reconstruction," 104; Berwanger, *West and Reconstruction,* 187. Theodore S. Greiner to Seward, September 11, 1865, NMTP, complained of the "shame" of regularly seeing Governor Connelly and his family "escorted by three or four Navajos . . . stolen in raids . . . and held as property."

5. *Heredia vs. Garcia,* SFWG, February 2, 1867.

6. Murphy, "Reconstruction," 103–110; Larry D. Ball, *The United States Marshals of New Mexico and Arizona Territories, 1846–1912* (Albuquerque: University of New Mexico Press, 1978), 51–52.

7. Murphy, "Reconstruction," 100–105.

8. Bernalillo County Docket Book, Judicial District 2, May 1867, 118–165, NMSRCA.

9. *Territory vs. Benjamin Kelsey, William Kelsey, and James A. Jeremiah,* Case

No. 346, May 10 and 13, 1867, and *Territory vs. William Kelsey,* Case No. 371, May 18, 1867, Bernalillo County Docket Book, 129–130, 133, 137, 162–163; testimony of Stephen B. Elkins, *William L. Rynerson vs. J. D. Sena, Sh'ff S.F. Co. upon Habeas Corpus,* SFNM, January 28, 1868.

10. Slough to Santiago Hubbell, June 30, 1867, Hubbell Family Papers, NMORCA. Slough had requested a three-month leave to begin May 1, 1867 and continue through the summer recess of courts in order to see to his wife's health and to find suitable schools for his children. The leave was granted, but Slough never took it, and his family remained with him in New Mexico. See Slough to Henry Stanbery, November 10, 1866, AGP.

11. Rec. 204, Case No. 95, July 31, 1867, and Case No. 97, August 1, 1867, *U.S. vs. Guadalupe Mares,* for "Selling liquor to Indians," July Term, First Judicial District, is summarized in the testimony of Peter Connelly, *Rynerson vs. Sena,* SFNM, January 28, 1868.

12. SFNM, August 10, 1867.

13. The problem of the Comancheros and the whiskey trade is examined in Kenner, *New Mexican–Plains Indian Relations,* 155–200.

14. Curiously, in spite of the considerable attention given to Indian affairs that summer and fall because of the work of the Indian Commission, this decision provoked no comment in the press.

15. Elkins to Stanbery, October 1, 1867, AGP; Indian Appropriation Act of February 27, 1851 (*U.S. Statutes at Large,* 9 [1851]: 587); Ball, *U.S. Marshals,* 252n.

16. Stanbery to Elkins, November 23, 1867, *Annual Report of the Commissioner of Indian Affairs, 1867* (Washington: GPO, 1867), 222. A copy of the Stanbery letter is also found in the Thomas B. Catron Papers, SCZL. See also Chaves to Heath, October 26, November 1, 1867, Chaves Letters.

17. Slough's opinion in the case of *Benigno Ortiz vs. the United States* was printed in full in the SFNM, August 3, 1867. This decision was subsequently upheld by the New Mexico Supreme Court in the case of *United States vs. Lucero,* 1 N.M. 422 (1869), opinion written by John S. Watts, Slough's successor. The U.S. Supreme Court affirmed the decision in the case of *United States vs. Joseph,* 94 U.S. 614 (1876). For a full discussion of the legal complications in relations between the Pueblo Indians and the United States, see Felix S. Cohen, *Handbook of Federal Indian Law* (Albuquerque: University of New Mexico Press, 1972), 383–400, especially 387–393. Also useful is G. Emlen Hall, "The Pueblo Grant Labyrinth," in *Land, Water, and Culture: New Perspectives on Hispanic Land Grants,* edited by Charles L. Briggs and John R. Van Ness (Albuquerque: University of New Mexico Press, 1987), 94–103. The decision provoked some criticism that Slough's action was politically motivated. SFWG, August 3, 1867; SFNM, August 10, 1867.

18. SFNM, August 10, 1867. See also SFWG, August 10, 1867, which declared that Slough had "all of the requisite qualifications for the speedy dispatch of business in court."

19. *Territory vs. Juan Jose Herrera,* San Miguel County Docket Book, 250–251, San Miguel County Court House, Las Vegas, New Mexico.

20. Testimony of Connelly, Elkins, Henry Henrie, R. H. Tompkins, and Severo

Baca, *Rynerson vs. Sena,* SFNM, January 28, 1868.

21. *Ibid.*

22. *Ibid.*

23. *Ibid.*

24. Testimony of Tompkins in *ibid.* Attorney General Merrill Ashurst concurred, but he argued that Slough was not partisan.

25. Floyd S. Fierman, "The Frontier Career of Charles Clever," *El Palacio,* 85 (Winter 1979–1980), 2–6, 34; Ball, *U.S. Marshals,* 23-24.

26. For extensive commentary on the election, see the files of the SFNM and the SFWG for September and October 1867.

27. Ball, *U.S. Marshals,* 52–53. Ball bases his account largely on *House Misc. Doc. No. 154,* 40th Cong., 2d sess. Also, *Papers in the Case of J. Francisco Chavez vs. Charles P. Clever, Delegate from the Territory of New Mexico, Santa Fe, October 1, 1867* (Washington: GPO, 1868), 92–95, 107–111, 129–131, 147–148, 157–161.

28. Chaves to Heath, December 11, 1867, Chaves Letters.

29. Executive Records of the Territory of New Mexico, 2: 2, September 20, 1867, NMTP. The entry reads, "The Governor this day issued a Certificate of Election to Chas P. Clever, as Delegate to Congress (to this Certificate the Secretary of the Territory protested in writing)."

30. Heath to Colfax, October 1, 1867, published in the SFWG, December 14, 1867.

31. Heath to Dawes, October 23, 1867, Heath Letterbook, 105–138.

32. Chaves to Heath, August 29, 1867, Chaves Letters.

33. Chaves to Heath, September 5, October 26, and November 1, *ibid.*

34. Chaves to Heath, October 26, *ibid.*

35. *Ibid.* See also Heath to Dawes, October 23, 1867, Heath to N. P. Chipman, December 24, 1867, and Heath to L. B. Flesh, February (?), 1868, Heath Letterbook, 105–138, 185–189, 244–247.

36. Chaves to Heath, November 1, 1867, Chaves Letters.

37. SFNM, October 19 and 26, November 5, 12, and 19, 1867.

38. Heath to Dawes, October 23, 1867, Heath Letterbook, 105–138.

39. *Ibid.* The most notable reference to Slough's sentiments was found in the SFWG, August 3, 1867, which reported in an article about the Pueblo decision that Slough was "in favor of the election of Gen'l. Clever."

40. Chaves to Heath, October 26, 1867, Chaves Letters. For a useful sketch of Brocchus, see Ralph Emerson Twitchell, "Address," *New Mexico Bar Association Minutes, 1895* (Santa Fe: New Mexico Bar Association, 1895), 18–23.

41. Chaves to Heath, October 26 and November 1, 1867, Chaves Letters.

Chapter 3

1. Bernalillo County Docket Book (Judicial District 2), October Term, 1867, 205, 210, 212–214, NMSRCA.

2. *Ibid.*, 213–214.

3. Testimony of Elkins, Henrie, Tompkins, Ashurst, Connelly, Baca, and Jose Sena, *Rynerson vs. Sena,* SFNM, January 28, 1868.

4. SFWG, October 5, 1867; SFNM, November 5, 1867.

5. SFWG, November 30, 1867.

6. Entry for December 2, 1868, Executive Record, NMTP; SFNM, December 3 and 10, 1867; SFWG, December 7, 1867.

7. SFNM, December 3, 1867.

8. Testimony of Thomas S. Tucker, *Rynerson vs. Sena,* SFNM, January 28, 1868.

9. *Ibid.*

10. Testimony of Eben Everett, *ibid.*

11. SFNM, December 3, 1867.

12. The motion to swear in the legislature was adopted on December 2, 1867, at which time the legislature, upon deciding to have Heath swear them in, recessed and went to find him. "Diario del Consejo Legislativo (Council Journal, 1865–1870, in Spanish)," 245, Papers of the Legislature, New Mexico Territory, 1867–68, Ter/c302, Box 2, SCZL; SFNM, December 3, 1867; SFWG, December 7, 1867; Heath to J. M. Binckley, December 7, 1867, AGP; J. L. Collins to the U.S. attorney general, R. Burns Folder, APDJ. For an especially interesting contemporary account by a visitor in Santa Fe, see M. A. to EDS. NEWS on December 6, 1867, DRMN, published December 17, 1867.

13. Testimony of I. D. Fuller, H. C. Carson, and Don Jesus Maria Pacheco, *Rynerson vs. Sena,* SFNM, January 28, 1868.

14. Testimony of Fuller, *ibid.*

15. *Ibid.* Fuller said that when someone referred to "General" Heath, Slough said, "General be damned, him a General, the damned cowardly son of a bitch."

16. *Ibid.;* Testimony of J. Howe Watts, preliminary examination before Judge Joab Houghton in the case of the *Territory of New Mexico vs. William L. Rynerson,* SFWG, January 11, 1868, and SFNM, January 14, 1867.

17. SFNM, December 3, 1867.

18. DRMN, December 17, 1867.

19. Heath to Rynerson, November 10 and 11, 1867, Heath Letterbook, 148–150; a copy of Heath's certificate, dated November 10, 1867, appears in NMTP. Lemon reviewed the election returns along with Probate Clerk J. F. Bennett, Dona Ana County Sheriff Mariano Barelo, and Evangelista Chavez, a justice of the peace. They threw out the votes of four precincts for irregularities and declared the vote to be 432 for Samuel Jones and 423 for Rynerson, Dona Ana County Probate Court Records, notes courtesy Jane C. Sanchez.

20. On December 2 the credentials committee reported all credentials in order except for those for Dona Ana County, noting that Jones had a certificate from John Lemon and Rynerson a certificate from Heath. "Hon. Candelerio Garcia . . . agreed to leave the credentials in contention until the matter might be legally decided." "Diario," 244. Diego Archuleta introduced a resolution that Jones be declared the senator-elect until the evidence could be examined. Don Jesus Maria Pacheco then made a motion that the resolution be referred to a special committee. On the following day, this committee reported its opinion that Rynerson was entitled to the seat. The motion to seat Jones was withdrawn, and Rynerson was permitted to take the seat until the matter was formally settled. Journal of the Legislative Council, 1867–1868, Folios 6–7, NMSRCA. On December 5 the Council declared Rynerson to be a legal member. Pacheco then moved that a three-man committee be designated to advise Rynerson "to come take his seat as a member of this body." This motion was adopted, and Pacheco, Andres Romero, and Felipe Sandoval brought Rynerson to the chamber, where he was sworn in by the probate judge of Santa Fe County and seated. "Diario," 254–257.

21. Darlis A. Miller, "William Logan Rynerson in New Mexico, 1862–1893," NMHR, XLVIII (1973): 101–131, is the best biographical treatment, although Miller's book, *The California Column in New Mexico* (Albuquerque: University of New Mexico Press, 1982), contains much additional material. Especially helpful was Jane C. Sanchez to GLR, February 8, 1971.

22. William L. Rynerson, CMSR, AGO. Other records for the Department of New Mexico, USAC, NA, RG 393, indicate that Rynerson had some difficulties while serving in the regiment in New Mexico.

23. Miller, *California Column,* 174–175.

24. "Diario" entry for December 4, 1867 (248), on motion of Don Jesus Maria Pacheco; DRMN, December 17, 1867. Samuel J. Jones explained his view of the controversy in a letter to New Mexicans, dated December 7, 1867, in the SFWG, December 28, 1867.

25. SFWG, December 14 and 21, 1867.

26. Heath to Colfax, October 1, 1867, SFWG, published December 14, 1867; Chaves to Heath, December 11, 1867, Chaves Letters.

27. DRMN, December 17, 1867.

28. SFWG, December 14, 1867.

29. *Ibid.* The *Gazette* carried the full proceedings of the meetings on December 3, 4, and 5, 1867, leading to the adoption of resolutions condemning Heath.

30. DRMN, December 17, 1867.

31. *Ibid.*

32. SFNM, December 10, 1867. See also the testimony of Antonio Ortiz y Salazar, *Rynerson vs. Sena.*

33. Slough to the public, December 4, 1867, published in SFWG on December 7, 1867.

34. Testimony of Carson, *Rynerson vs. Sena.*

35. SFWG, December 7, and 14, 1867. A printed copy of the resolution endorsing Heath is included in Heath's File, APDJ.

36. SFNM, December 10, 1867; Heath to Binckley, December 7, 1867, AGP.

37. *Ibid.* Acts and Memorials of the Assembly, Ter/c301, Box 1.

38. Heath to Binckley, December 7, 1867, AGP.

39. See Pacheco's affidavit, dated February 12, 1868, and published in the SFWG, May 2, 1868. See also the testimony of Joseph Purcell, Connelly, Henrie, and Elkins, *Rynerson vs. Sena,* SFNM, January 28, 1868; and the SFWG, December 21, 1867.

40. The testimony of Purcell, Connelly, Henrie, and Elkins in *Rynerson vs. Sena,* SFNM, January 28, 1868, illuminates both the questions asked by Rynerson and the kinds of answers he received.

41. Entry for December 7, 1867, "Diario," 261.

42. SFNM, December 10, 1867.

43. A hand-written copy of the resolution is among the Assembly Papers, Ter/c301, Box 2, SCZL. The printed resolution, with an endorsement by Heath, is filed in Heath's folder, APDJ.

44. Testimony of Elkins, Ashurst, and Connelly, *Rynerson vs. Sena,* January 28, 1868.

45. Entries for December 11, 12, and 14, 1867, "Diario," 274–279.

46. Entry for December 14, *ibid.* Only Sanchez and Juan Andres Martinez voted against the resolutions. Heath's endorsement is on the printed resolutions against Slough, Heath File, APDJ.

47. Testimony of Carson, Wilder, Capt. Little, and S. B. Wheelock, *New Mexico vs. Rynerson,* SFWG, January 11, 1868, and SFNM, January 14, 1868. See also Heath to Binckley, December 17, 1867, APDJ.

48. Testimony of Carson and McDonald, *New Mexico vs. Rynerson,* SFWG, January 11, 1868, and SFNM, January 14, 1868.

49. Testimony of McDonald, *ibid.*

50. Testimony of Ashurst and Wheelock, *ibid.*

51. Testimony of Reverend McFarland and Connelly, *Rynerson vs. Sena,* SFNM, January 28, 1868.

52. Testimony of McDonald, Samuel Duncan, and Daniel Tappan, *New Mexico vs. Rynerson,* SFWG, January 11, 1868, and SFNM, January 14, 1868. Curiously, Duncan was the law partner of H. H. Heath, a fact that makes the subject of his conversation with Slough all the more tantalizing.

53. Collins to the attorney general, December 15, 1867, APDJ.

54. Testimony of Col. Francisco Abreu, *Rynerson vs. Sena,* SFNM, January 28, 1868.

55. This account of the shooting is reconstructed from the testimony of Tappan, McDonald, Duncan, Stevens, Hubbell, Conway, Jacob Gold, and Van C. Smith, *New Mexico vs. Rynerson.* SFWG, January 11, 1868, and SFNM, January 14,

1868.

56. Testimony of Dr. McKee, Dr. Kennon, McDonald, Tappan, Hubbell, and Smith, *ibid.*

57. SFWG, December 21, 1867; Clarendon to Editor, December 24, 1867, Cincinnati *Commercial,* published December 29, 1867; Meketa, *Legacy of Honor,* 313.

58. This incident was kept out of the newspapers, but Rafael Chacon noted it in his diary. See Meketa, *Legacy of Honor,* 313.

Chapter 4

1. Collins to attorney general, December 15, 1867, APDJ.

2. Endorsement on *ibid.*

3. Mitchell to Stanbery, December 17, 1867, AGP.

4. Clever to Stanbery, December 28, 1867, AGP.

5. SFWG, December 21, 1867.

6. Collins to attorney general, December 15, 1867, APDJ.

7. Clever to William H. Seward, January 2, 1867, NMTP.

8. Clever to Stanbery, December 28, 1867, AGP.

9. Clever to Seward, January 2, 1867, NMTP.

10. SFWG, December 21 and 28, 1867, January 4, 11, and 18, 1868.

11. *Ibid.* January 18, 1868.

12. "The Preambles and Resolutions unanimously adopted by a Mass Meeting of Santa Fe County, held on the 19th day of January 1868, in the city of Santa Fe," NMTP.

13. Heath to N. P. Chipman, December 24, 1867, Heath Letterbook, 185–189. See also his letters to F. N. Seward on December 23, 1867, Chaves on December 30, 1867, and Maj. L. B. Flesh on February 2, 1868, 182–184, 196–203, 244–247.

14. Mitchell, "To the Presidents of the Council," December 30, 1867, from Legislative Assembly Papers, NMSRCA, reprinted in full in Sanchez, "'agitated'" 217–218. See also the series of memorials and laws vetoed by Mitchell, in the Territorial Papers of the United States Senate, Segregated File, New Mexico, Tray 2, NA, RG 46, and Acts and Memorials of the Assembly, Ter/c301, Box 1, 2, SCZL. One law vetoed by Mitchell that has implications connected to Slough was a law to provide for the selection of jurors.

15. Clever to Stanbery, December 28, 1867, and Clever to Johnson, January 27, 1868, AGP.

16. See especially "A Card to the People of New Mexico," written anonymously by "Vox Populi," SFWG, January 4, 1867. The writer especially attacked the Radical pretensions of Chaves, Heath, and company, noting particularly the prevalence of pro-peonage men in the ranks of the Chaves-Heath faction. He

declared, "If Chavez is a 'Radical' then is Vallandingham [the most notorious congressional Copperhead during the war] one too — and that a strong one." The same issue of the *Gazette* carried Samuel Jones's detailed review of his dispute with Rynerson over the council seat. He charged that Heath had usurped the territory's election laws and taken it upon himself to ignore the voters of New Mexico and "to decide who shall compose their legislature and who shall rule over them as their civil officers." See also other issues of the *Gazette* for January and February 1868. On January 4, for example, the paper reported that Clever had been seated by the House of Representatives and used the occasion to attack Heath and the legislature, "the majority of whom are perfectly adapted to the use and service of demagogues." On January 25, Editor Russell wrote a blistering editorial concerning the peonage question and accused Chaves and Heath of hypocrisy.

17. Heath to Binckley, January 17, 1867, APDJ.

18. Elkins to Stanbery, December 22, 1867, AGP.

19. SFNM, December 24, 1867.

20. Cincinnati *Commercial,* December 29, 1867.

21. Cincinnati *Commercial,* January 3, 1868. Heath wrote a response on January 18, published in the *Commercial* on January 27, 1868, in which he vociferously denied charges of complicity in Slough's death and declared that he was unaware of the troubles between Slough and Rynerson until Governor Mitchell told him about the shooting on the afternoon of the incident. On January 21 the *New Mexican* published the letter along with an angry editorial vowing to expose its author. On March 3, 1868, the paper identified Watts as the author and published Heath's letter to the *Commercial* as well. The same day, Heath wrote a letter concerning his intention of suing the editors of the *Commercial.* He also sought to have Watts removed from military service, calling him an "active Copperhead" and accusing him of "offensively acting the partisan at the Polls, at elections with his shoulder straps on." Heath to William B. Sheppard, March 3, 1868; Heath to Senator Henry Wilson, March 24, 1868, Heath Letterbook, 313–314; 409–411. J. Howe Watts was the son of Judge Watts, a point Heath made certain to note.

22. Council Bluffs (Iowa) *Nonpareil,* quoted in SFWG, February 1, 1868.

23. Dubuque (Iowa) *Herald,* quoted in SFWG, January 25, 1868.

24. Atchison (Kansas) *Champion,* quoted in *ibid.*

25. Heath to Chipman, December 24, 1867, Heath Letterbook, 185–189. See also Heath's letters to F. N. Seward, December 23, 1867, to Chaves, December 30, 1867, and to Maj. L. B. Flesh, February 2, 1868, Letterbook, 182–184, 196–203, 244–247.

26. SFWG, January 18, 1867; Chaves to Heath, December 11, 1867, and January 4 and 8, 1868, Chaves Letters, provide the gist of Chaves's arguments, although the telegram itself has not been found. As early as December 11, Chaves had written Heath, "All your friends and mine regret that you did not from the beginning take the responsibility and give me a clean certificate without any explanation."

27. Heath to Chaves, December 30, 1867, Heath Letterbook, 196–203.

28. Chaves to Stanbery, January 2, 1868, AGP; Chaves to Heath, January 4, 1868, Chaves Letters. See also the extended notes entitled "Chief Justice of New Mexico," dated January 18, 1868, which summarize the correspondence with the Justice Department on the subject, in AGP.

29. Chaves to Heath, January 8, 1868, Chaves Papers.

30. *Ibid.,* January 4.

31. *Ibid.,* December 11, 1867, and January 8, 1868. See also Heath to Governor (?) on January 29, 1868, Heath to Chaves on February 28, 1868, and Heath to Brocchus on March 19, 1868, in the Heath Letterbook, 236–238, 301–303, 379–381. Full details of the activities of Benedict and Elkins are found in *Chaves vs. Clever: Papers and Evidence,* 1–183, *passim; House Mis. Doc. No. 14,* 40th Cong., 3rd Sess., *Chaves vs. Clever: Additional Papers in the Case of J. F. Chaves against C. P. Clever of New Mexico* (Washington: GPO, 1869), 1–43; and *House Report No. 18,* 40th Cong., 3rd Sess., *J. F. Chaves vs. C. P. Clever* (Washington: GPO, 1869), 1–5.

32. Heath to Arny, January 6, 1868, quoted in Heath to Chaves, March 17, 1868, Heath Letterbook, 361–365; entries for December 31, 1867, and January 2, 11, 14, and 20, 1868, "Diario," 307–312, 327–328, 332–335, and 242–243. See also Sanchez, " 'agitated' " 220–221.

33. Sanchez, " 'agitated' " 221–223, provides the most easily accessible copy of the resolutions. Other copies are found in the Assembly Papers, NMSRCA, and in NMTP. The precipitating factor was a letter written by Mitchell to the "Presidents of the Council and the House of Representatives," December 30, 1867, in the Assembly Papers. See also a series of laws and memorials vetoed by Mitchell in the Territorial Papers of the United States Senate, Segregated File, New Mexico, Tray 2, NA, RG 46.

34. See Heath to Arny, January 6, 1868, quoted in Heath to Chaves, March 17, 1868, Heath Letterbook, 361–365. Heath was too discreet. He advised Arny, "I must be kept in the background as an applicant for the Governorship. You know that my appointment would give delight to *our people;* but I will not apply, *myself, now!*" Arny inferred from the letter that Heath was not interested in the appointment and so advised Chaves and others, much to Heath's consternation.

35. Sanchez, " 'agitated' " 223–227, conveniently summarizes these proceedings. Notably, the chairman of this committee was William Logan Rynerson. On January 19, 1868, at a mass meeting in Santa Fe, resolutions were adopted defending Mitchell and calling for the removal of Heath. See Merrill Ashurst, Jose Manuel Gallegos, and Antonio Sena to Andrew Johnson, January 22, 1868, transmitting the resolutions, NMTP. See also the account in SFWG on January 25, 1868.

36. Elkins to Chaves, January 25 and March 10, 1868, Arny to Stanbery, January 15, 1868, Brocchus File, APDJ; Chaves to Heath, February 24, 1868, Chaves Letters.

37. SFWG, January 18, 1868. That same day, the legislative council passed a resolution to adjourn for Slough's funeral and tabled the resolutions it had passed the previous Friday. However, the council took care to state "that it is not the intention of the Council to concede, nor in any manner to suspend its

acts by fear, lies, favor, partiality, or lack of probity; but only by finding the said Superior Judge in the agony of death." Translation from Journal of the Legislative Council, Folio 9, NMSRCA.

38. The testimony that follows is taken from reports of the proceedings of *New Mexico vs. Rynerson* in SFWG, January 11, 1868, and SFNM, January 14, 1868.

39. SFWG, January 11, 1868.

40. SFNM, January 14, 1868.

41. *Ibid.* This information did not come from the testimony before Judge Houghton. Its source was not given.

42. Again, the source of this statement was not provided by the *New Mexican.*

43. SFNM, January 14, 1868.

44. *Ibid.* See also the letter of "Argus" to the Editor of the *New Mexican,* dated January 19, 1868 and published in SFNM on February 11, 1868, and Heath to Binckley, January 13, 1868, APDJ, for other attacks on Houghton.

45. SFWG, January 18, 1868.

46. *Ibid.* See also SFNM, February 18, 1868. Heath even accused Houghton of not living in the territory in violation of his oath. Heath to Binckley, January 13, 1868, APDJ.

47. Heath to Binckley, January 13, 1868, APDJ.

48. *Rynerson vs. Sena,* SFNM, January 28, 1868. As early as December 30, 1867, the Legislative Council had passed a resolution demanding to know why Rynerson was being held "without any examination which is conceded by the law." Journal of the Legislative Council, Folio 4, NMSRCA.

49. Summary of preliminary motions, *Rynerson vs. Sena,* SFNM, January 28, 1868.

50. *Ibid.* Allowing the testimony of a preliminary hearing to stand as testimony-in-chief in another proceeding was highly irregular in the first place, but it also meant that cross-examination on points of fact in the case was virtually eliminated. The focus of the *habeas corpus* hearing now shifted away entirely from the circumstances under which Rynerson shot Slough.

51. Meketa, *Legacy of Honor,* 312–313. Chacon was the senator from Taos County during 1865–1866. He was replaced in 1867–1868 by Don Jesus Maria Pacheco, but he served as "principle secretary" for the Legislative Council during the latter term. Of this experience, Chacon noted, "I found occasion to mix myself up in the politics of New Mexico . . . and there I was able to note, to my great disillusionment, the political manipulations in which honor and dignity were sold and respectability forgotten."

52. The officers were not called to corroborate this testimony. See also the testimony of Don Anastacio Sandoval, *Rynerson vs. Sena,* January 28, 1868.

53. Tucker attributed Slough's resignation specifically to the Mares case, but he testified that Slough also alluded to other episodes in which Mitchell had pardoned felons without consulting him. *Rynerson vs. Sena,* SFNM, January 28, 1868.

54. Testimony of Elkins, *Rynerson vs. Sena,* SFNM, January 28, 1868. This particular letter has not been located.

55. Preliminary hearings of the period were notoriously lax in the standards of evidence applied. Because these hearings were held to determine whether sufficient evidence existed to hold a prisoner for trial, attorneys sought primarily to elicit information; little effort was made to impugn witnesses. That would wait for trial.

56. Bond was posted within half an hour after Brocchus handed down his decision, "and Col. Rynerson went forth a free man." So said the SFNM on January 28, 1868, adding, "The best men in the Territory offered themselves as bondsmen." The actual bond shows Anastacio Sandoval, Celso Baca, Severo Baca, Stephen B. Elkins, John Gorgan, Jr., and Kirby Benedict as sureties. *Territory of New Mexico vs. William L. Rynerson,* Case File No. 180a, Santa Fe County District Court Records, NMSRCA.

57. Ashurst to attorney general, January 28, 1868, APDJ.

58. SFNM, January 28, 1868.

59. *Weekly Arizonian,* reprinted in SFNM, February 18, 1868.

60. Mitchell and Collins to attorney general, January 29, 1868, APDJ.

61. Ashurst to attorney general, January 28, 1868, *ibid.*

62. Arny actually went to Washington to assist Chaves; SFWG, January 4, 1868, and Elkins to Chaves, January 25, *ibid.* Speaking of Brocchus to Boniface Chaves, the brother of Jose Francisco Chaves, Heath said, "Heaven could not have sent a more direct blessing upon this people. . . . I am certain that justice was never administered with more purity than he administers it." Heath Letterbook, 321–323.

63. Heath to Governor (?), January 29, Heath Letterbook, 236–238.

Chapter 5

1. SFNM, January 14, 1868.

2. Mrs. John P. Slough to Salmon P. Chase, February 18, 1868, APDJ.

3. A. C. McLean to Stanbery, February 3, 1868, *ibid.*

4. Poldervaart, *Black-Robed Justice,* 71. On May 9, 1868, the SFWG reported that Army surgeon J. C. McKee had supervised the exhumation of Slough's remains, which were placed in "a walnut box lined with zinc" and shipped east to Cincinnati and a final resting place there.

5. A true bill was returned on March 3, 1868, *Territory of New Mexico vs. William L. Rynerson,* NMSRCA. The case against Rynerson was originally filed as Case No. 175a. This case was dismissed on March 3, 1868, then refiled under Case No. 180a, based on the Grand Jury indictment. Information from Susie M. Montoya, District Court Clerk, First Judicial District, Santa Fe, to GLR, June 28, 1972.

6. See the summary of proceedings filed by Peter Connelly, Chief Clerk, March 9, 1868, in *Territory of New Mexico vs. William L. Rynerson.*

7. *Ibid.* See also Rynerson affidavit dated March 6, 1868, in the same file, and the criminal docket, Record Book, 1867–1870, 84–86.

8. Motion of Ashurst regarding witnesses, March 17, 1868, in *ibid.*

9. Motion of Ashurst for change of venue, March 17, 1868, *ibid.*

10. N.D.L. to Editors, *New Mexican,* March 23, 1868, and SFNM, April 7, 1868.

11. *Ibid.*

12. Heath to Rynerson, March 19, 1868, Heath Letterbook, 387.

13. N.D.L. to Editors, March 23, 1868, SFNM, published April 7, 1868; Case No. 159, *Territory vs. William L. Rynerson,* District Court Record Book, 1866–1868, San Miguel County District Court Records, 379–380, NMSRCA.

14. N.D.L. to Editors, March 23, 1868, SFNM, published April 7, 1868.

15. "Charge of His Honor, Perry E. Brocchus in the Case of Col. W. L. Rynerson," SFNM, April 7, 1868.

16. Heath to Henrie, March 21, 1868, Heath Letterbook, 389–391.

17. N.D.L. to Editors, March 23, 1868, SFNM, published April 7, 1868.

18. *Ibid.,* March 24, 1868.

19. SFWG, March 21, 1868.

20. SFNM, March 31, 1868. See also the DRMN, April 3, 1868, which reported that the verdict was received favorably in New Mexico.

21. Heath to Brocchus, March 22, 1868, Heath Letterbook, 393–395.

22. Heath to John M. Thayer, April 8, 1868, *ibid.,* 446–449.

23. Heath to Chaves, March 17, 1868, *ibid.,* 361–365. See also Heath to Col. Chas. E. Moss, April 11, *ibid.,* 481–483, in which Heath states, "I know that the leaders as well as the masses of the party desire and expect my appointment for Governor. Col. Chaves has been anxious for this & is so now. If you know what I had passed through here, in the incipient efforts to establish a Republican *Party,* where only a Republican element heretofore existed; how, in pursuit of my principles, my life has been endangered months at a time here, *you* would be for me too." Moss was being promoted for governor of New Mexico by William Breeden, and Heath offered him a position as associate justice of the territorial Supreme Court instead.

24. Chaves to Heath, February 24 and April 3, 1868, Chaves Letters; Heath to Chaves, March 26, 1868, Heath Letterbook, 425–426. Heath's conversion to Radical principles was vocal, if not sincere. All of his letters in March and April were filled with references to "Andy Johnsonism" and impeachment. See Heath to Chaves, March 17 and 19, 1868, Heath to Hawkins Taylor, March 24, 1868, Heath to Thayer, April 8, 1868, Heath to L. W. Lipton, April 8, 1868, and Heath to Rynerson, April 12, 1868, Heath Letterbook, 361–365, 382–385, 412–414, 446–449, 450–452, and 489–490.

25. Chaves to Heath, January 8 and February 24, 1868, Chaves Letters.

26. Heath to Hawkins Taylor, March 24, 1868, Heath Letterbook, 412–414.

27. Heath to Harlan, April 8, 1868, *ibid.,* 455–458.

28. Heath to Thayer, April 8, 1868, and Heath to L. W. Lipton, April 8, 1868, *ibid.,* 446–449, 450–452.

29. Clever to Seward, January 2, March 7, 10, 11, 14, and April 8, 1868, with appended petitions, NMTP.

30. Clever to Seward, March 7, 1868; affidavit of Don Jesus Maria Pacheco, February 5, 1868, *ibid.*

31. Heath to Henrie, March 21, 1868, Heath Letterbook, 389–391. See also Mitchell to Seward on March 7, Heath to Seward on March 8, Heath to Seward (telegram) on March 8, Heath to Chaves on March 8, William Lilly to Seward on March 22, and Heath to Seward, April 16, all 1868, NMTP. In his March 8 letter to Chaves, Heath accused Mitchell and Clever of a "low trick." "You know what Mitchell will be at when he gets there," he wrote.

32. Heath to Rynerson, April 12, 1868, Heath Letterbook, 489–490.

33. In March, the *Gazette* turned its attention to other matters and downplayed the ongoing feud until Watts had been nominated; when that announcement came, the *Gazette* rejoined the fray. SFWG, March 21, 28, and April 4, 11, 18, 1868. The *New Mexican* was more aggressive during this period. See SFNM, April 7 and 14, 1868.

34. SFNM, April 14, 1868.

35. SFWG, April 18, 1868.

36. SFNM, April 21, 1868.

37. SFWG, April 25, 1868.

38. SFNM, April 28, 1868.

39. Twitchell, "Address," 20–21. See SFNM, May 5, 1868, for yet another defense of Brocchus.

40. SFWG, May 2, 1868.

41. *Ibid.* In the same issue, the *Gazette* belittled the notion of the *New Mexican* as a Radical paper. "It goes as the organ of the radicals in New Mexico, but the radicals and republicans do not acknowledge it as their organ. They oppose peonage. It does not. They oppose Indian slavery. It does not. They favor the execution of the laws of Congress abolishing both these institutions. It does not. They are in favor of keeping up with the spirit of the times in every respect. It holds on to Mexican foggyisms of the sixteenth century."

42. SFNM, May 12, 1868. On May 5, 1868, the SFNM finally published an Iowa newspaper report defending Heath. The article from the Washington (Iowa) *Press,* originally published on April 8, called Heath a "gallant Iowa soldier" and declared that when other Republican papers criticized him, they "know not what they do."

43. Chaves to Heath, June 15, 1868, Chaves Letters.

44. Clever to Johnson, June 15, 1868, NMTP.

45. Schofield to Seward, June 26, 1868, and Heath to Offutt, April 9, 1861, Bureau

of Claims Report, June 30, *ibid.*

46. Heath to Offutt, April 9, 1861, certified copy in *ibid.*

47. SFWG, July 18, 1868. The *Gazette* printed the letter again on October 10, 1868, and January 16, 1869. Notably, the *New Mexican* never attempted to explain the letter, choosing rather to ignore it entirely.

48. Chaves to Heath, June 15, 1868, Chaves Letters. Unfortunately, the Heath Letterbook ends in April 1868, so that Heath's response to the Offutt letter disclosure is sketchy at best.

49. Chaves to Heath, June 23, *ibid.* Chaves told Heath flatly, "From all that I can gather it appears that it is the intention of the President to supercede you with Bergman." Edward H. Bergman was an associate of Clever's from Santa Fe. See Clever's letter to Johnson, June 16, 1868, NMTP, which followed immediately upon the heels of Clever's disclosure of the Offutt letter.

50. Brocchus to Seward, August 21, 1868, quoting from Heath's letter to him, NMTP, NA, RG 60.

51. Poldervaart, *Black-Robed Justice,* 78–80.

52. SFNM, February 6, 1869.

53. Poldervaart, *Black-Robed Justice,* 81–83.

54. SFNM, February 23, 1869. See also the issue for February 16, 1869.

55. Heath to Seward, November 26, 1868, February 2 and 4, 1869; Heath to Mitchell, February 2, 1869; Mitchell to Heath, February 4, 1869; Mitchell to Seward, February 28, 1869, NMTP. On March 30, 1869, Mitchell resigned, effective "from the date of the qualification of my successor." Grant appointed C. C. Crowe, an ex-Confederate, to Mitchell's post on April 3, but he did not qualify. See Horn, *Troubled Years,* 130.

56. SFNM, February 16, 1869; Poldervaart, *Black-Robed Justice,* 83; Twitchell, *Leading Facts,* 2: 399–401. By then the letters and editorials were flowing freely again; almost every issue of the *Gazette* and *New Mexican* contains some reference.

57. Perkins to Hamilton Fish, May 6, 1869, NMTP.

58. Heath to Fish, May 24, 1869, *ibid.* The secretary of state advised Heath that the governor would serve "until his successor shall be appointed and qualified unless sooner removed by the President." Mitchell, like Heath, continued to create problems. He declared war on the Navajos and Gila Apaches late in his tenure, causing protests from practically every group and agency in New Mexico and Washington. This doubtlessly speeded his departure. See Horn, *Troubled Years,* 130–131.

59. Pile to Grant, April 30 and May 7, 1870; Pile et al., to Lyman Trumbull, April 9, 1870, NMTP. See also Ball, *U.S. Marshals,* 61–62.

60. SFNM, August 30, 1870, reprinted in Oliver La Farge, *Santa Fe: The Autobiography of a Southwestern Town* (Norman: University of Oklahoma Press, 1959), 70–71.

61. Ware, *Indian War of 1864,* 96. No application for pension was ever filed with the Veteran's Bureau by the wife or family of Heath, leaving his last years

something of a mystery.

62. Lamar, *Far Southwest,* 135.

63. *Ibid.,* 136–170; and Larson, "Territorial Politics," 254–258, provide the most balanced views, although by no means the only interpretations.

64. Keleher, *Turmoil in New Mexico,* 484n.

65. Miller, "Rynerson," 105–113.

66. Miller, *California Column,* 180–182.

67. *Ibid.,* 183; Twitchell, *Leading Facts,* 3: 203–206.

68. Miller, "Rynerson," 111; Jane C. Sanchez to GLR, February 8, 1971.

69. Miller, in both "Rynerson," 113–115, and *California Column,* 217–219, discusses Rynerson's role in the Lincoln County War. For other assessments see Maurice Garland Fulton, *The History of the Lincoln County War* (Tucson: University of Arizona Press, 1968), William A. Keleher, *Violence in Lincoln County, 1869–1881* (Albuquerque: University of New Mexico Press, 1957); and Robert M. Utley, *High Noon in Lincoln: Violence on the Western Frontier* (Albuquerque: University of New Mexico Press, 1987), all of which give somewhat less than flattering views of Rynerson.

70. Miller, "Rynerson," 115–126; Arrell Morgan Gibson, *The Life and Death of Colonel Albert Jennings Fountain* (Norman: University of Oklahoma Press, 1965), 175–211.

Chapter 6

1. The literature is vast. Basic sources include Fulton, *Lincoln County War;* William A. Keleher, *Maxwell Land Grant: A New Mexico Item* (Santa Fe: Rydal Press, 1942); Keleher, *Violence in Lincoln County;* Jim B. Pearson, *The Maxwell Land Grant* (Norman: University of Oklahoma Press, 1961); Morris F. Taylor, *O. P. McMains and the Maxwell Land Grant Conflict* (Tucson: University of Arizona Press, 1979); and Utley, *High Noon.* Useful articles include Jack DeMattos, "John Kinney," *Real West,* 27 (February 1984): 20–25; Robert N. Mullin, "Here Lies John Kinney," *Journal of Arizona History,* 14 (Autumn, 1973): 223–242; and several articles by Philip J. Rasch: "John Kinney: King of the Rustlers," *English Westerners Brand Book,* 4 (October 1951): 10–12; "The Horrell War," NMHR, 31 (1956): 223–231, "The Pecos War," *Panhandle-Plains Historical Review,* 29 (1956): 101–111; "The Murder of Juan Patron," *Potomac Westerners Corral Dust,* (July, 1960): 20–21; "The Rustler War," NMHR, XXXIX (1964): 257–273; and "The Tularosa Ditch War," NMHR, XXXXIII (1968): 229–235. Also see Lee Scott Theisen, editor, "Frank Warner Angel's Notes on New Mexico Territory, 1878," ARW, 18 (1970): 333–370; Miller, *California Column,* 63–78, 101–118; and Rosenbaum, *Mexicano Resistance,* 68–98.

2. Larson, *Quest for Statehood,* 138–139; Taylor, *McMains and Maxwell Land Grant, passim;* Norman Cleaveland with George Fitzpatrick, *The Morleys — Young Upstarts on the Southwest Frontier* (Albuquerque: Calvin Horn Publishers, Inc., 1971), 72–147.

3. Thiesen, "Angel's Notes," 333–337; Westphall, *Catron,* 122–134.

4. H. L. Nieburg, in his book *Political Violence: The Behavioral Process* (New York: St. Martin's Press, 1969), 13, defines political violence as "acts of disruption, destruction, injury whose purpose, choice of targets or victims, surrounding circumstances, implementation, and/or effects have political significance, that is, tend to modify the behavior of others in a bargaining situation that has consequences for the social system." Nieburg's definition and analysis influenced the interpretation presented here.

5. See also Rasch, "Murder of Patron," 20–21; Fulton, *Lincoln County War,* 405–409; and Rosenbaum, *Mexicano Resistance,* 99–124. Norman Cleaveland, grandson of William Morley, is convinced his grandfather was assassinated by Santa Fe Ring associates, despite contemporary reports that the incident was an accident. See especially his *A Synopsis of the Great New Mexico Cover-Up* (privately printed, 1989), *passim.*

6. Charles H. Lange and Carroll L. Riley, editors, *The Southwestern Journals of Adolph F. Bandelier, 1883–1884* (Albuquerque: University of New Mexico Press, 1970), 380; Lamar, *Far Southwest,* 192–193.

7. Tobias Duran, "Francisco Chavez, Thomas B. Catron, and Organized Political Violence in Santa Fe in the 1890s," NMHR, 59 (1984): 291–310; Lamar, *Far Southwest,* 193.

8. Lamar, *Far Southwest,* 192–195; Ball, *U.S. Marshals,* 151–155; Westphall, *Catron,* 210–216. Ball refers to the murder of John Doherty as "the most senseless" of the many assassinations of the period.

9. Rosenbaum, *Mexicano Resistance,* 99–124; Robert W. Larson, "The White Caps of New Mexico: A Study of Ethnic Militancy in the Southwest," *Pacific Historical Review,* 44 (1975): 171–185. Rosenbaum and Larson collaborated in an excellent analysis, "Mexicano Resistance to the Expropriation of Grant Lands," 269–310. They note, at p. 275, that after 1870, *Mexicanos* found it increasingly difficult to act within the *modus vivendi* because Anglos infringed directly on their ways of life.

10. Gibson, *Albert Jennings Fountain,* 192–281; Leon C. Metz, *Pat Garrett: The Story of a Western Lawman* (Norman: University of Oklahoma Press, 1974), 133–153.

11. Keleher, *Turmoil in New Mexico,* 481n.

12. Don Cline, "The Murder of Pat Garrett," *Quarterly of the National Association and Center for Outlaw and Lawman History,* XIII (1989): 19–23; Don Cline, "Pat Garrett's Tragic Lawsuit," *Old West,* 25 (Summer, 1989): 18–23; James Madison Hervey, "The Assassination of Pat Garrett," *True West,* 8 (March–April, 1061): 42; Metz, *Garrett,* 229–251; Robert N. Mullin, *The Strange Story of Wayne Brazel* (Canyon, Texas: Palo Duro Press, 1969); Robert N. Mullin, "The Key to the Mystery of Pat Garrett," *Los Angles Westerners Corral Branding Iron,* (June, 1969): 1–5; Colin W. Rickards, *How Pat Garrett Died* (Santa Fe: Palomino Press, 1970), *passim;* and Glenn Shirley, *Shotgun for Hire: The Story of "Deacon" Jim Miller, Killer of Pat Garrett* (Norman: University of Oklahoma Press, 1970), 74–91.

13. Rosenbaum and Larson, "Mexicano Resistance to the Expropriation of Grant Lands," 295–300; James Rowen, "Quick Triggers in New Mexico," *The Nation,*

(June 19, 1972), 781–783. See also Patricia Bell Blawis, *Tijerina and the Land Grants: Mexican Americans Struggle for Their Heritage* (New York: International Publishers, 1971); Richard Gardner, *Grito! Reies Tijerina and the New Mexico Land Grant War of 1967* (New York: Harper Colophon Books, 1971); and Peter Nabokov, *Tijerina and the Courthouse Raid* (Albuquerque: University of New Mexico Press, 1970), for discussions of a modern episode of violence with ethnic overtones.

14. Joe B. Frantz, "The Frontier Tradition: An Invitation to Violence," in Graham and Gurr, eds., *Violence in America*, 1: 101–120; Gary L. Roberts, "The West's Gunmen: II," *America West*, 8 (March, 1971), 61–62, and "Violence and the Frontier Tradition," *Kansas and the West: Bicentennial Essays in Honor of Nyle H. Miller*, edited by Forest R. Blackburn et al. (Topeka: Kansas State Historical Society, 1976), 96–111.

15. Kirkham et al., *Assassination and Political Violence*, 38–40.

16. *Ibid.*, 9–43; Utley, *High Noon*, 177.

17. For an introduction to this period see Ray Ginger, *Age of Excess: The United States from 1877 to 1914* (New York: The Macmillan Company, 1965) and Robert H. Weibe, *The Search for Order* (New York: Hill and Wang, 1967). For a more specific look, see Robert V. Bruce, *1877: Year of Violence* (Chicago: Quadrangle Books, 1959).

18. Richard Slotkin, *The Fatal Environment: The Myth of the Frontier in the Age of Industrialization, 1800–1890* (New York: Atheneum, 1985), 60–62; Nieburg, *Political Violence, 13–16.* See also Louise Charles and Richard Tilly, *The Rebellious Century, 1830–1930* (Cambridge: Harvard University Press, 1975), and William A. Gamson, *The Strategy of Social Protest* (Homewood, Illinois: Dorsey Press, 1975).

19. Roberts, "Violence and Frontier Tradition," 107.

20. Slotkin, *Fatal Environment*, 284–290.

21. Kent L. Steckmesser, *The Western Hero in History and Legend* (Norman: University of Oklahoma Press, 1965). See also Brown, *Strain of Violence*, 3–36; Frantz, "Frontier Tradition," 1: 101–120; and Roberts, "West's Gunmen: II," 61–62. Gilded Age newspapers in virtually every locale featured with great regularity stories about homicides and other violent confrontations.

22. Wichita (Kansas) *Eagle*, May 20, 1875.

23. San Antonio (Texas) *Express*, March 14, 1876.

24. Edith Abbott, "The Civil War and the Crime Wave of 1865–70," *Social Science Review*, 1 (June, 1927): 215–229. See also Robert V. Hine, *The American West: An Interpretive History*, 2d ed. (Boston: Little, Brown and Company, 1984), 333–338.

25. Richard White, "Outlaw Gangs of the Middle Border: American Social Bandits," WHQ, 12 (1981): 387–408; Michael Fellman, *Inside War: The Guerilla Conflict in Missouri During the American Civil War* (New York: Oxford University Press, 1989), 231–266; and Paul I. Wellman, *A Dynasty of Western Outlaws*, Bison Edition (Lincoln: University of Nebraska Press), 1986.

26. Slotkin, *Fatal Environment*, 291–294, 309–316.

27. The standard works on Southern honor are John Hope Franklin, *The Militant South* (Boston: Beacon Press, 1966); and Bertram Wyatt-Brown, *Southern Honor: Ethics and Behavior in the Old South* (New York: Oxford University Press, 1982). On the "code of the west" see C. L. Sonnichsen, *I'll Die Before I'll Run: The Story of the Great Feuds of Texas* (New York: Devin-Adair Company, 1962), 3–13; and Utley, *High Noon,* 176–178. For evidence of the role of honor elsewhere, see Gerald F. Linderman's provocative book, *Embattled Courage: The Experience of Combat in the American Civil War* (New York: The Free Press, 1987), *passim;* and Elliott J. Gorn's useful article, "'Good-Bye Boys, I Die a True American': Homicide, Nativism, and Working-Class Culture in Antebellum New York City," JAH, 74 (1987): 388–410.

28. Linderman, *Embattled Courage,* 7–12. See also Elliott J. Gorn, *The Manly Art: Bare-Knuckle Prize Fighting in America* (Ithaca: Cornell Unversity Press, 1986), 138–140.

29. Linderman, *Embattled Courage,* 12; Gorn, "'Good-Bye Boys,'" 403.

30. Historians tend to specialize and to assume that conditions found in the areas of their specialties are unique, which is sometimes true. However, the differences are occasionally exaggerated. The concept of honor in the nineteenth century seems to suffer from this.

31. White, "Outlaw Gangs," 397–408.

32. SFNM, January 14, 1868; SFWG, January 18, 1868.

33. Richard Maxwell Brown, "'Meet Anyone Face to Face' and Keep the Bullet in Front," MMWH, 37 (Summer, 1987): 74.

34. *Ibid.,* 75.

35. Quoted in Philip D. Jordan, *Frontier Law and Order: Ten Essays* (Lincoln: University of Nebraska Press, 1970), 9–10.

36. Sonnichsen, *I'll Die Before I'll Run,* 8–9.

37. Quoted in Brown, "Keep the Bullet in Front," 74–75.

38. Quoted in Gary L. Roberts, "The Wells Spicer Decision: 1881," MMWH, 20 (January, 1970): 70. See also John P. Clum, *It All Happened at Tombstone* (Flagstaff: Northland Press, 1965), 11, for a similar point of view by a contemporary of the Earps.

39. Quoted in Brown, "Keep the Bullet in Front," 76.

40. Roberts, "Violence and the Frontier Tradition," 103–105.

41. Manuel Romero to Aniceto Salazar, December 24, 1867, SFWG, published January 25, 1868. The reference to the "nest of Jews" underscored a certain anti-Semitism toward the community of Jewish merchants in Santa Fe. Heath shared this attitude. In a letter to Chaves dated February 28, 1868, Heath wrote in reference to Clever, "As to the *Jew from New Mexico,* he acted about as honorably as I could have expected." Heath Letterbook, 301–303. See also Parrish, "The German Jew . . . in New Mexico," *passim.*

42. Holmes, *Politics in New Mexico,* 19. For comparisons to other territories, see Lamar, *Far Southwest.*

43. Rosenbaum and Larson, "Mexicano Resistance to the Expropriation of Grant

Lands," 269–270, 278–291; and Seligmann, "Withdrawal," 4–8. See also Alvin R. Sunseri, *Seeds of Discord: New Mexico in the Aftermath of American Conquest, 1846–1861* (Chicago: Nelson-Hall, 1979), 125–135, for useful background information.

44. Utley, *High Noon,* 174–175.

45. Prince statement quoted in Duran, "Political Violence in Santa Fe," 294. See Westphall, *Catron,* 209, for example of efforts to blame violence on "bad" Mexicans.

46. See Kirkham et al., *Assassination and Political Violence,* 5–6, for comments on the pre-conditions for assassination.

47. Rosenbaum, *Mexicano Resistance,* 140–157.

48. Rosenbaum and Larson, "Mexicano Resistance to the Expropriation of Grant Lands," 285–295.

49. *La Voz del Pueblo,* October 15, 1892, quoted in Duran, "Political Violence in Santa Fe," 299.

50. Duran, "Political Violence in Santa Fe," 295–305.

51. *Ibid.,* 300–307.

52. Heath to F. N. Seward, December 23, 1867, Heath Letterbook, 182–184.

53. Prince to Victor L. Ochoa, July 22, 1892, quoted in Lamar, *Far Southwest,* 192.

54. Roberts, "Violence and the Frontier Tradition," 109.

55. No single work adequately examines the nature of the political order in the territorial period. Westphall's *Catron* deals with that important leader; Lamar, *Far Southwest,* offers a survey; and Larson, "Territorial Politics and Cultural Impact," considers the cultural dimension.

56. Roberts, "Violence and the Frontier Tradition," 105.

57. Crotty, "Assassinations and Their Interpretation," 25.

58. Lamar, *Far Southwest,* 198–200; Holmes, *Politics in New Mexico,* 43–60, 145–146, 175–176. Otero solidified Republican control so completely that even Democrats like Albert Bacon Fall switched parties. Yet, after 1910, fortunes gradually shifted to the Democrats and to the progressive wing of the Republican party.

59. Holmes, *Politics in New Mexico,* 43–60; Lamar, *Far Southwest,* 171–201; Larson, *Quest for Statehood, passim.*

60. The differences with Arizona are striking. See Jay J. Wagoner, *Arizona Territory, 1863–1912: A Political History* (Tucson: University of Arizona Press, 1970).

61. SFNM, July 12, 1876, quoted in Poldervaart, *Black-Robed Justice,* 99.

62. *Ibid.*

63. SFNM, February 26, 1877 in *ibid.,* 100.

64. *Ibid.,* 97–98.

65. Utley, *High Noon,* 53–54.

66. Poldervaart, *Black-Robed Justice,* 155–178; Westphall, *Catron,* 208–229.

67. Wagoner, *Arizona Territory,* 191–200; and Paula Mitchell Marks, *And Die in the West: The Story of the O.K. Corral Gunfight* (New York: William Morrow and Company, Inc., 1989).

68. Brown, *Strain of Violence,* 236–299.

69. *Ibid.,* 15; Sonnichsen, *I'll Die Before I'll Run, passim.*

70. Lamar, *Far Southwest,* 171–201; Rosenbaum, *Mexicano Resistance,* 140–153.

71. Prince to John W. Noble, April 23, 1892, quoted in Lamar, *Far Southwest,* 196.

72. Nieburg, *Political Violence,* 47–73, provides a useful model of the bargaining process and how it degenerates into violence.

73. *Ibid.,* 53–56, demonstrates the differences between legality (technical and formal rules that provide the form of law) and legitimacy (the underlying consensus that gives — or denies — government real power).

Bibliography

Primary Sources

Manuscript Collections

Charles Anderson Papers. Cincinnati Historical Society, Cincinnati, Ohio.

William F.M. Arny Letterbook. William G. Ritch Collection, Henry E. Huntington Library and Art Gallery, San Marino, California.

Hiram Pitt Bennet to John P. Slough, January 30, 1865. Western Americana Collection, Yale University Library, New Haven, Connecticut.

Thomas B. Catron Papers. Special Collections. Zimmerman Library, University of New Mexico, Albuquerque, New Mexico.

Jose Francisco Chaves Letters. Arizona Historical Society, Tucson, Arizona.

William H. Gilpin Collection. Chicago Historical Society, Chicago, Illinois.

John A. Halderman Collection. Kansas State Historical Society, Topeka, Kansas.

Herman H. Heath Letterbook, 1867–1868. Special Collections, Zimmerman Library, University of New Mexico, Albuquerque, New Mexico.

Hubbell Family Papers. New Mexico State Records Center and Archives, Santa Fe, New Mexico.

Letters and Other Manuscript Materials Written by J. M. Chivington, S. F. Tappan, L. N. Tappan, J. P. Slough, E. W. Wynkoop, et al., between the Years 1861 and 1869. Microfilm Copy, Colorado Historical Society, Denver.

William H. Seward Papers. University of Rochester Library, Rochester, New York.

National Archives

Adjutant General's Office, Record Group 94.
    Compiled Military Service Records of Volunteer Soldiers: Herman H. Heath, Robert B. Mitchell, William L. Rynerson, and John P. Slough.
    General,s Papers.
    Letters Received, General Files.

Department of Justice, Record Group 60.
    Appointment Papers.
    General Records.
    Attorney general's Papers.

Department of State, Record Group 59.
    General Records.
    Letters of Application, Lincoln and Johnson.
    New Mexico Territorial Papers.

United States Senate, Record Group 46
    Territorial Papers, Segregated File, New Mexico, Tray 2.

Other Public Records

Acts and Memorials of the Assembly, 1867–1868, Papers of the Legislature, New
    Mexico Territory, Ter/c302, Box 1, Special Collections, Zimmerman Library,
    University of New Mexico, Albuquerque.
Assembly Papers, 1867–1868, Papers of the Legislature, New Mexico Territory,
    Ter/c302, Box 2, Special Collections, Zimmerman Library, University of New
    Mexico, Albuquerque.
Bernalillo County Docket Book, 1866–1867, New Mexico State Records Center and
    Archives, Santa Fe.
Criminal Docket, Record Book, 1867–1870, Santa Fe County District Court Records,
    New Mexico State Records Center and Archives, Santa Fe.
"Diario del Consejo Legislativo (Council Journal, 1865–1870, in Spanish)," Papers of
    the Legislature, New Mexico Territory, 1867–1868, Ter/c302, Box 2, Special
    Collections, Zimmerman Library, University of New Mexico, Albuquerque.
Dona Ana County Probate Court Records, Dona Ana County Courthouse, Las
    Cruces, New Mexico (notes courtesy Jane C. Sanchez).
Journal of the Legislative Council, 1867–1868, New Mexico State Records Center
    and Archives, Santa Fe.
San Miguel County Docket Book, 1866–1868, San Miguel County Court House, Las
    Vegas, New Mexico.
Territory of New Mexico vs. William L. Rynerson, Case File No. 180a, Santa Fe
    County District Court Records, New Mexico State Records Center and Ar-
    chives, Santa Fe.
Territory of New Mexico vs. William L. Rynerson, District Court Record Book,
    1866–1868, San Miguel County District Court Records, New Mexico State
    Records Center and Archives, Santa Fe.

Government Documents

Annual Report of the Commissioner of Indian Affairs, 1867. Washington: Govern-
    ment Printing Office, 1867.
House Misc. Doc. No. 154, 40th Cong. 2d Sess., *Papers in the Case of J. Francisco
    Chavez vs. Charles P. Clever, Delegate from the Territory of New Mexico, Santa
    Fe, October 1, 1867.* Washington: Government Printing Office, 1868.
House Misc. Doc. No. 14, 40th Cong. 3rd Sess., *Chaves vs. Clever: Additional Papers
    in the Case of J. F. Chaves against C. P. Clever of New Mexico.* Washington:
    Government Printing Office, 1869.
House Report No. 18, 40th Cong. 3rd Sess., *J. F. Chaves vs. C. P. Clever.* Washington:
    Government Printing Office, 1869.
*Journal of the House of Representatives of the State of Ohio, Being the Second
    Session of the Fifty-Second General Assembly Commencing on Monday, Janu-
    ary 5, 1857.* Columbus: Statesman Steam Press, 1857.
U.S. Statutes at Large.

Newspapers

Cincinnati (Ohio) *Commercial.*
Cincinnati (Ohio) *Gazette.*
Cleveland (Ohio) *Leader.*
Columbus (Ohio) *Gazette.*
Denver (Colorado) *Daily Rocky Mountain News.*
Santa Fe (New Mexico) *New Mexican.*
Santa Fe (New Mexico) *Weekly Gazette.*
Washington (D.C.) *Daily National Intelligencer.*
Wichita (Kansas) *Eagle.*
San Antonio (Texas) *Express.*

Books and Periodicals

Clum, John P., *It All Happened at Tombstone.* Edited by John D. Gilchriese. Flagstaff: Northland Press, 1965.
Hervey, James Madison, "The Assassination of Pat Garrett," *True West,* 8 (March–April, 1961): 17, 40–42.
Hollister, Ovando J., *Boldly They Rode: A History of the First Colorado Regiment of Volunteers.* Lakewood, Colorado: The Golden Press, 1949.
LaFarge, Oliver, *Santa Fe: The Autobiography of a Southwestern Town.* Norman: University of Oklahoma Press, 1959.
Lange, Charles H., and Carroll L. Riley, editors, *The Southwestern Journals of Adolph F. Bandelier, 1883–1884.* Albuquerque: University of New Mexico Press, 1970.
Meketa, Jacqueline Dorgan, *Legacy of Honor: The Life of Rafael Chacon, A Nineteenth Century New Mexican.* Albuquerque: University of New Mexico Press, 1986.
Notices of the House of Representatives of the State of Ohio in the Fifty-Second General Assembly, Convened January 7th, 1856. Columbus: N.p. 1857.
Theisen, Lee Scott, editor, "Frank Warner Angel's Notes on New Mexico Territory, 1878," *Arizona and the West,* 18 (1970): 333–370.
Ware, Eugene F., *The Indian War of 1864.* Edited by Clyde G. Walton. Bison Edition. Lincoln: University of Nebraska Press, 1960.

Secondary Sources

Books

Bailey, L. R., *Indian Slave Trade in the Southwest: A Study of Slave-Taking and the Traffic of Indian Captives.* Los Angeles: Westernlore Press, 1966.
Ball, Larry D., *The United States Marshals of New Mexico and Arizona Territories, 1846–1912.* Albuquerque: University of New Mexico Press, 1978.

Beck, Warren A., *New Mexico: A History of Four Centuries*. Norman: University of Oklahoma Press, 1962.

Berwanger, Eugene H., *The West and Reconstruction*. Urbana: University of Illinois Press, 1981.

Blawis, Patricia Bell, *Tijerina and the Land Grants: Mexican Americans Struggle for Their Heritage*. New York: International Publishers, 1971.

Briggs, Charles L., and John R. Van Ness, editors, *Land, Water, and Culture: New Perspectives on Hispanic Land Grants*. Albuquerque: University of New Mexico Press, 1987.

Brown, Richard Maxwell, *Strain of Violence: Historical Studies of American Violence and Vigilantism*. New York: Oxford University Press, 1975.

Bruce, Robert V., *1877: Year of Violence*. Chicago: Quadrangle Books, 1959.

Charles, Louise, and Richard Tilly, *The Rebellious Century, 1830–1930*. Cambridge: Harvard University Press, 1975.

Cleaveland, Norman, with George Fitzpatrick, *The Morleys — Young Upstarts on the Southwest Frontier*. Albuquerque: Calvin Horn Publishers, Inc., 1971.

——, *A Synopsis of the Great New Mexico Cover-Up*. Privately printed, 1989.

Cohen, Felix S., *Handbook of Federal Indian Law*. Albuquerque: University of New Mexico Press, 1972.

Colton, Ray C., *Civil War in the Western Territories*. Norman: University of Oklahoma Press, 1959.

Crotty, William J., editor, *Assassinations and the Political Order*. New York: Harper & Row, 1971.

Current, Richard Nelson, *Those Terrible Carpetbaggers: A Reinterpretation*. New York: Oxford University Press, 1988.

Dunning, William A., *Reconstruction, Political and Economic*. [1907] New York: Harper & Row, 1962.

Eisenschiml, Otto, *The Celebrated Case of Fitz-John Porter: An American Dreyfus Affair*. Indianapolis: Bobbs-Merrill Co., 1950.

Espinosa, J. Manuel, *Crusaders of the Rio Grande*. Chicago: Institute of Jesuit History, 1942.

Fellman, Michael, *Inside War: The Guerilla Conflict in Missouri During the American Civil War*. New York: Oxford University Press, 1989.

Foner, Eric, *Reconstruction: America's Unfinished Revolution, 1863–1877*. New York: Harper & Row, 1988.

Forbes, Jack, *Apache, Navajo, and Spaniard*. Norman: University of Oklahoma Press, 1960.

Franklin, John Hope, *The Militant South*. Boston: Beacon Press, 1966.

Fulton, Maurice Garland, *The History of the Lincoln County War*. Edited by Robert N. Mullin. Tucson: University of Arizona Press, 1968.

Gamson, William A., *The Strategy of Social Protest*. Homewood, Illinois: Dorsey Press, 1975.

Gardner, Richard, *Grito! Reies Tijerina and the New Mexico Land Grant War of 1967*. New York: Harper Colophon Books, 1971.

Gibson, Arrell Morgan, *The Life and Death of Colonel Albert Jennings Fountain*. Norman: University of Oklahoma Press, 1965.

Ginger, Ray, *Age of Excess: The United States from 1877 to 1914*. New York: The Macmillan Company, 1965.

Gorn, Elliott J., *The Manly Art: Bare-Knuckle Prize Fighting in America*. Ithaca: Cornell University Press, 1986.

Graham, Hugh Davis, and Ted Robert Gurr, editors, *Violence in America: Historical and Comparative Perspectives.* 2 vols. Washington: Government Printing Office, 1969.

Hackett, Charles W., *Revolt of the Pueblo Indians of New Mexico and Otermin's Attempted Reconquest, 1680–1682.* Albuquerque: University of New Mexico Press, 1942.

Hall, Martin H., *Sibley's New Mexico Campaign.* Austin: University of Texas Press, 1960.

Hine, Robert V., *The American West: An Interpretive History.* 2d ed. Boston: Little, Brown and Company, 1984.

Holmes, Jack E., *Politics in New Mexico.* Albuquerque: University of New Mexico Press, 1967.

Horgan, Paul, *The Great River: The Rio Grande in North American History.* 2 vols. New York: Holt, Rinehart & Winston, 1954.

Horn, Calvin A., *New Mexico's Troubled Years: The Story of the Early Territorial Governors.* Albuquerque: Horn & Wallace, 1963.

Hunt, Aurora, *Major General James H. Carleton, 1814–1873: Western Frontier Dragoon.* Glendale: Arthur H. Clark Co., 1958.

———, *Kirby Benedict: Frontier Judge.* Glendale: Arthur H. Clark Co., 1961.

Jones, Oakah L., Jr., *Pueblo Warriors & Spanish Conquest.* Norman: University of Oklahoma Press, 1966.

Jordan, Philip D., *Frontier Law and Order: Ten Essays.* Lincoln: University of Nebraska Press, 1970.

Keleher, William A., *Maxwell Land Grant: A New Mexico Item.* Santa Fe: Rydal Press, 1942.

———, *Turmoil in New Mexico, 1846–1868.* Albuquerque: University of New Mexico Press, 1986.

———, *Violence in Lincoln County, 1869–1881.* Albuquerque: University of New Mexico Press, 1957.

Kelly, Lawrence C., *Navajo Roundup.* Boulder: Pruett Press, 1970.

Kenner, Charles L., *A History of New Mexican–Plains Indian Relations.* Norman: University of Oklahoma Press, 1969.

Kirkham, James F., Sheldon G. Levy, and William J. Crotty, *Assassination and Political Violence: A Report to the National Commission on the Causes and Prevention of Violence.* Washington: Government Printing Office, 1969.

Lamar, Howard Roberts, *The Far Southwest, 1846–1912: A Territorial History.* New Haven: Yale University Press, 1967.

Larson, Robert W., *New Mexico's Quest for Statehood.* Albuquerque: University of New Mexico Press, 1968.

Lavender, David, *Bent's Fort.* New York: Doubleday, 1954.

LeCompte, Janet, *Rebellion in Rio Arriba, 1837.* Albuquerque: University of New Mexico Press, 1985.

Linderman, Gerald R., *Embattled Courage: The Experience of Combat in the American Civil War.* New York: The Free Press, 1987.

McNitt, Frank, *Navajo Wars: Military Campaigns, Slave Raids and Reprisals.* Albuquerque: University of New Mexico Press, 1972.

Marks, Paula Mitchell, *And Die in the West: The Story of the O.K. Corral Gunfight.* New York: William Morrow and Company, Inc., 1989.

Metz, Leon C., *Pat Garrett: The Story of a Western Lawman.* Norman: University of Oklahoma Press, 1974.

Miller, Darlis A., *The California Column in New Mexico.* Albuquerque: University of New Mexico Press, 1982.

Mullin, Robert N., *The Strange Story of Wayne Brazel.* Canyon, Texas: Palo Duro Press, 1969.

Murphy, Lawrence R., *Frontier Crusader — William F.M. Arny.* Tucson: University of Arizona Press, 1972.

Nabokov, Peter, *Tijerina and the Courthouse Raid.* Albuquerque: Unversity of New Mexico Press, 1970.

Nieburg, H. L., *Political Violence: The Behavioral Process.* New York: St. Martin's Press, 1969.

Pearson, Jim B., *The Maxwell Land Grant.* Norman: University of Oklahoma Press, 1961.

Perrigo, Lynn L., *The American Southwest: Its People and Cultures.* New York: Holt, Rinehart & Winston, 1971.

Poldervaart, Arie, *Black-Robed Justice.* Santa Fe: Historical Society of New Mexico, 1949.

Rickards, Colin W., *How Pat Garrett Died.* Santa Fe: Palomino Press, 1970.

Rosenbaum, Robert J., *Mexicano Resistance in the Southwest: "The Sacred Right of Self Preservation."* Austin: University of Texas Press, 1981.

St. John, Elizabeth A.H., *Storms Brewed in Other Men's Worlds: The Confrontation of Indians, Spanish, and French in the Southwest, 1540–1795.* College Station: Texas A & M University Press, 1975.

Shirley, Glenn, *Shotgun for Hire: The Story of "Deacon" Jim Miller, Killer of Pat Garrett.* Norman: University of Oklahoma Press, 1970.

Simmons, Marc, *Murder on the Santa Fe Trail: An International Incident, 1843.* El Paso: Texas Western Press, 1986.

Slotkin, Richard, *The Fatal Environment: The Myth of the Frontier in the Age of Industrialization, 1800–1890.* New York: Atheneum, 1985.

Sonnichsen, C. L., *I'll Die Before I'll Run: The Story of the Great Feuds of Texas.* New York: Devin-Adair Company, 1962.

Spicer, Edward H., *Cycles of Conquest: The Impact of Spain, Mexico, and the United States on the Indians of the Southwest, 1533–1960.* Tucson: University of Arizona Press, 1962.

Steckmesser, Kent L., *The Western Hero in History and Legend.* Norman: University of Oklahoma Press, 1965.

Stratton, Porter A., *The Territorial Press of New Mexico.* Albuquerque: University of New Mexico Press, 1969.

Sunseri, Alvin R., *Seeds of Discord: New Mexico in the Aftermath of American Conquest, 1846–1861.* Chicago: Nelson-Hall, 1979.

Taylor, Morris F., *O. P. McMains and the Maxwell Land Grant Conflict.* Tucson: University of Arizona Press, 1979.

Thompson, Gerald, *The Army and the Navajo: The Bosque Redondo Reservation Experiment, 1863–1868.* Tucson: University of Arizona Press, 1976.

Thrapp, Dan L., *The Conquest of Apacheria.* Norman: University of Oklahoma Press, 1967.

Trafzer, Clifford E., *The Kit Carson Campaign: The Last Great Navajo War.* Norman: University of Oklahoma Press, 1982.

Twitchell, Ralph Emerson, *Leading Facts of New Mexican History.* New edition. 2 vols. Albuquerque: Horn &Wallace, 1963.

———, *Old Santa Fe.* Chicago: Rio Grande Press, 1963.

Utley, Robert M., *High Noon in Lincoln: Violence on the Western Frontier.* Albuquerque: University of New Mexico Press, 1987.

Wagoner, Jay J., *Arizona Territory, 1863–1912: A Political History.* Tucson: University of Arizona Press, 1970.

Walter, Paul A.F., Frank W. Clancy, and M. A. Otero, *Colonel Jose Francisco Chaves, 1833–1904.* Santa Fe: Historical Society of New Mexico Papers, 1926.

Warner, Ezra J., *Generals in Blue.* Baton Rouge: Louisiana State University Press, 1964.

Weber, David J., *The Mexican Frontier, 1821–1846: The American Southwest Under Mexico.* Albuquerque: University of New Mexico Press, 1982.

Weibe, Robert H., *The Search for Order.* New York: Hill and Wang, 1967.

Wellman, Paul I., *A Dynasty of Western Outlaws.* Bison Edition. Lincoln: University of Nebraska Press, 1986.

Westphall, Victor, *Thomas Benton Catron and His Era.* Tucson: University of Arizona Press, 1973.

Wyatt-Brown, Bertram, *Southern Honor: Ethics and Behavior in the Old South.* New York: Oxford University Press, 1982.

Periodicals

Abbott, Edith, "The Civil War and the Crime Wave of 1865–70," *Social Science Review,* 1 (June 1927), 212–234.

Brown, Richard Maxwell, " 'Meet Anyone Face to Face' and Keep the Bullet in Front," *Montana, the Magazine of Western History,* 37 (Summer 1987): 74–76.

Cline, Don, "The Murder of Pat Garrett," *Quarterly of the National Association and Center for Outlaw and Lawman History,* XIII (1989): 19–23.

———, "Pat Garrett's Tragic Lawsuit," *OldWest,* 25 (Summer 1989): 18–23.

DeMattos, Jack, "John Kinney," *Real West,* 27 (February 1984): 20–25.

Duran, Tobias, "Francisco Chavez, Thomas B. Catron, and Organized Political Violence in Santa Fe in the 1890s," *New Mexico Historical Review,* XXXXXIX (1984): 291–310.

Fierman, Floyd S., "The Frontier Career of Charles Clever," *El Palacio,* 85 (Winter 1979–1980): 2–6, 34.

Gorn, Elliott J., " 'Good-Bye Boys, I Die a True American': Homicide, Nativism, and Working-Class Culture in Antebellum New York City," *Journal of American History,* 74 (1987): 388–410.

Larson, Robert W., "Territorial Politics and Cultural Impact," *New Mexico Historical Review,* XXXXXX (1985): 249–269.

———, "The White Caps of New Mexico: A Study of Ethnic Militancy in the Southwest," *Pacific Historical Review,* 44 (1975): 171–185.

McClure, Charles R., "The Texan–Santa Fe Expedition," *New Mexico Historical Review,* XXXXVIII (1973): 45–56.

Miller, Darlis A., "Hispanos in the Civil War in New Mexico: A Reconstruction," *New Mexico Historical Review,* XXXXXIV (1979): 105–123.

———, "William Logan Rynerson in New Mexico, 1862–1893," *New Mexico Historical Review,* XLVIII (1973): 101–131.

Mullin, Robert N., "Here Lies John Kinney," *Journal of Arizona History,* 14 (1973): 223–242.

———, "The Key to the Mystery of Pat Garrett," *Los Angeles Westerners Corral Branding Iron* (June 1969): 1–5.

Murphy, Lawrence R., "Reconstruction in New Mexico," *New Mexico Historical Review*, XLIII (1968): 99–115.

———, "William F. M. Arny: Secretary of New Mexico, 1862–1867," *Arizona and the West*, VIII (1966): 323–338.

Owings, Kenneth N., "Patterns and Structure in Western Territorial Politics," *Western Historical Quarterly*, I (1970): 373–392.

Parrish, William J., "The German Jew and the Commercial Revolution in Territorial New Mexico, 1850–1900," *New Mexico Historical Review*, XXXV (1960): 1–23, 129–141.

Perdue, Rosa M., "The Sources of the Constitution of Kansas," *Kansas Historical Collections*, VII (1902): 130–151.

Rasch, Philip J., "The Horrell War," *New Mexico Historical Review*, XXXI (1956): 223–231.

———, "John Kinney: King of the Rustlers," *English Westerners Brand Book*, 4 (October 1951): 10–12.

———, "The Murder of Juan Patron," *Potomac Westerners Corral Dust* (July 1960): 20-21.

———, "The Pecos War," *Panhandle-Plains Historical Review*, 29 (1956): 101–111.

———, "The Rustler War," *New Mexico Historical Review*, XXXIX (1964): 257–273.

———, "The Tularosa Ditch War," *New Mexico Historical Review*, XXXXIII (1968): 229–235.

Roberts, Gary L., "The Wells Spicer Decision: 1881," *Montana, the Magazine of Western History*, 20 (January 1970): 62–74.

———, "The West's Gunmen: II," *America West*, 8 (March 1971): 18–23, 61–62.

———, "Violence and the Frontier Tradition," *Kansas and the West: Bicentennial Essays in Honor of Nyle H. Miller.* Edited by Forest R. Blackburn et al. Topeka: Kansas State Historical Society, 1976, 96–111.

Rowen, James, "Quick Triggers in New Mexico," *The Nation* (June 19, 1972): 781–783.

Sanchez, Jane C., " 'agitated, personal, and unsound . . .' " *New Mexico Historical Review*, XLI (1966): 217–230.

"Sketch of the Career of General Robert B. Mitchell" [1895], *Kansas Historical Collections*, XVI (1925), 632–637.

Stephenson, Wendell H., "Robert Byington Mitchell," *Dictionary of American Biography.* 10 vols. Edited by Dumas Malone. New York: Charles Scribner's Sons, 1928–1937.

Tegeder, Vincent G., "Lincoln and the Territorial Patronage: The Ascendancy of the Radicals in the West," *Mississippi Valley Historical Review*, XXXV (1948): 77–90.

Twitchell, Ralph Emerson, "Address," *New Mexico Bar Association.* Santa Fe: New Mexico Bar Association, 1895, 18–23.

Waldrip, William I., "New Mexico During the Civil War," *New Mexico Historical Review*, XXVIII (1953): 163–182.

Westphall, David, "The Battle of Glorieta Pass: Its Importance in the Civil War," *New Mexico Historical Review*, XLIV (1969): 137–154.

White, Richard, "Outlaw Gangs of the Middle Border: American Social Bandits," *Western Historical Quarterly*, 12 (1981): 387–408.

Wright, Arthur A., "Colonel John P. Slough and the New Mexico Campaign," *Colorado Magazine*, XXXIX (1962): 89–105.

Unpublished Dissertations and Papers:

Roberts, Gary L., "Sand Creek: Tragedy and Symbol." Unpublished Ph.D. dissertation, Norman: University of Oklahoma, 1984.

————, "The Slough-Rynerson Quarrel: Political Violence in New Mexico, 1867." Unpublished paper presented at the Yale Conference of the Western History Association, 1972.

Seligmann, G. L., "Withdrawal: A *Mexicano* Response to Anglo Intrusion in 19th Century New Mexico." Unpublished paper of a study in progress, 1988.

Index